D0077928

Perspectives On
CAMPUS PLANNING

Meeting the Challenges of Purpose and Place

DOBER LIDSKY MATHEY
Arthur J. Lidsky, AICP, FAAAS
George G. Mathey, AICP

Published By:

385 Concord Avenue, Suite 201
Belmont, MA 02478-3096
T 617-489-1162
F 617-484-1595
www.dlmplanners.com

© 2015 DOBER LIDSKY MATHEY
Arthur J. Lidsky and George G. Mathey

ISBN 978-0-9964546-0-5

Book and Jacket design: Yvonne Santos

CONTENTS

INTRODUCTION

DOBER LIDSKY MATHEY (DLM) provides campus and facility planning for colleges, universities, and independent schools. We are a planning firm—*that is all we do*. It is what distinguishes us from architectural firms who also provide planning services but whose main focus is building design. We believe, and our clients believe, that this difference makes our planning more objective and more comprehensive. DLM's participatory planning process, environmental mapping techniques, and benchmarking database are part of an array of decision-making tools used to help clients improve their facilities and celebrate the unique purpose and sense of place shaping their campuses. To date, DLM has served over 400 schools, colleges, and universities worldwide and has applied those experiences and skills developed in years of work to many other types of educational, cultural, and scientific institutions.

In 2004 Dober Lidsky Mathey decided to issue a quarterly (sometimes trimonthly) set of ideas called Perspectives on Campus Planning. This book is a collection of the best of those ideas.

Additionally, several other white papers and published articles about campus and facility planning have been included. The book is divided into nine sections:

- Vision, Strategy, Priorities
- Organizing for Planning
- Campus Planning
- Standards, Tools, Guidelines
- Facilities Planning
- Student Life
- Town Gown Relations
- Academic Issues
- Miscellaneous Stuff

The first two sections focus on the beginning stages of planning, who should be involved, and suggestions on how an institution should prepare to start the process. The third section is about the process of campus planning. The focus of the remaining six sections is on various aspects of college and university planning.

Higher Education is changing, as it has since the 14th Century. Sometimes the change has been slow and subtle and at other times, change has been rapid and not subtle, like today. From technology to pedagogy, from finances to operations, and from students to campus life, higher ed is very different from the way it was just a decade ago.

These articles and writings reflect our reactions, observations, and perspectives on the changes that are relentlessly emerging. We hope you find these helpful as you work to guide your institution to an ever-brighter future.

PART ONE

VISION, STRATEGY, PRIORITIES

CHAPTER 1

"Prioritizing the Campus Agenda"

~ George G. Mathey, 2005

If a campus or facility plan lacking priorities is no true plan, how best to set priorities that bring structure, logic, and impetus to link the plan's initiatives into a compelling manifesto for improvement?

The most appropriate set of priorities will be found in the institution's academic, strategic, and financial planning. The principles guiding these plans should also direct the physical planning, otherwise building a case to present to supporters will be compromised. Without priorities rooted in the school's mission and the goals it has set for fulfilling that mission, planning and plan implementation becomes *ad hoc* and aimlessly opportunistic.

For institutions endowed with strong leadership that confidently and continuously integrates the various planning strands, leaders set the standard, which others generally rally to.

Of course, many colleges lack such planning acuity, and the priority-setting process should be methodical, or run the risk of devolving into a timid reflection of the views of those who are most: persuasive, loud, persistent, or cantankerous.

A methodical process involves evaluating each proposed project in regard to how well it advances the institution's strategic goals. If no formal, current statement of these goals exists, develop a working set during the campus planning effort.

Start this task early in the process since a participatory, iterative approach requires sufficient time to produce a goals statement the majority will embrace.

∗ ∗ ∗

"Most Strategic Plans are Neither Strategic Nor Plans"~ Arthur J. Lidsky, 2006

Most college and university strategic plans are neither strategic nor plans. Part vision, part wishful thinking, these documents are more public relations than institutional planning guides.

Yet, good, comprehensive campus planning depends upon a valid and well done strategic plan—for, without it, campus planning is *ad hoc*.

Mission Versus Vision

Whereas a mission statement describes what the college or university does—its *raison d'être*, a vision statement describes what the institution wishes to become or do—a statement of aspirations.

The strategic plan should achieve the vision, realize aspirations, and describe the various academic, financial, and programmatic initiatives required to do so. The key, then, is the vision—usually missing and usually misunderstood.

One of the simplest vision statements is from Clemson University: *Clemson will, in ten years, be one of the top 20 public research universities in the country*. At the time of that statement, Clemson was ranked in the top 30 by US News and World Reports. The University certainly had other goals, but this statement had significant financial, facilities, and programmatic implications and helped structure the planning process.

Another example is: *John Carroll University aspires to be a leader in science and mathematics education, known for pedagogical innovation, personal attention to students, and its positive impact on the surrounding community*.

A paragraph or two is all that is needed. A multi-page vision statement will not be concise and will more than likely blur the boundaries between vision, strategic planning, and public relations.

The Strategic Plan: The strategic plan should have the following components and characteristics: An institutional vision statement.

- Vision statement themes. Theme goals strategies for realizing the goals a time frame for achieving the goals—usually 10 to 15 years. Resources required—financial faculty and staffing, facilities, etc

- Identification of who is responsible for managing the plan and who is responsible for each strategy

Themes: One way to structure the strategic plan is to define a series of themes or topic areas that further define and support the vision. So, for instance, one theme might focus on student attraction and retention. Another might focus on undergraduate research, and a third might address pedagogy.

Each theme should have a series of goals that respond to the vision statement. Having a goal that states that "we will be a leader in undergraduate education" is meaningless if it is not stated in a way that is measurable. Broad, poorly defined goals are a common problem with college and university plans.

Strategies: Once the vision, themes, and goals have been articulated, the next step is the development of strategies to achieve the goals. Strategies are action oriented—they describe the various ways in which the institution intends to address a goal.

The person or office responsible for each strategy should be noted. One person from within the president's cabinet should be responsible for managing and realizing the strategic plan. A time frame and schedule should be established and needed resources identified.

Prioritization: Probably the most difficult aspect of the strategic planning process is prioritization. Not all of the strategies and initiatives can or should be realized at once. The institutional vision is for the next fifteen years. One approach is to decide what can and should be accomplished in the next five year blocks, with a check for progress every five years to adjust vision, goals, and strategies.

The strategic planning process is an important institutional management tool. Do it seriously and do it well. In a future article, I will discuss how to organize the process.

* * *

"Managing Expectations"

~ George G. Mathey, 2009

When we initiate planning studies—discussing process, deliverables and desired results with our clients, we are often asked, "How will your process manage expectations?" Many campus leaders are clearly concerned that a participatory planning process can open a can of worms by encouraging faculty, staff and students to think "too big", resulting in a planning agenda far too ambitious for the institution's limited capital dollars. As the planning proceeds, we are just as often surprised to uncover the opposite problem—that of thinking "too small". Most of the campus user representatives we speak to have a highly-refined sense of institutional capabilities, and often are focused simply on "fixing what's broken" and not on re-inventing, or transforming their campus.

In practice, one hallmark of the participatory planning model is that when you truly engage a client group, it strengthens a sense of shared responsibility and a realistic understanding of what's possible in the planning horizon under discussion.

To realize this benefit of participation, several steps should be taken starting prior to the active process and ending after the final report is complete:

Plan for Planning

- Identify **all** the individuals that need to be engaged.
- Identify **all** possible existing campus groups that should be

DLM Staff

University of Massachusetts Lowell (UMass Lowell), Lowell, MA
South Campus Forum

involved in the planning. Think about which of these groups are essential to the process and need to be repeatedly engaged, as opposed to those who are tangential to the process but would appreciate an opportunity for input.

- Seek to engage these groups more than once in the process. If the groups or individuals are essential, expect three sessions as a minimum for true engagement—an initial meeting to introduce the process and schedule and gather preliminary input, a second to present major findings and gather feedback, and a third for confirmation of the proposed recommendations and commentary.

During the Planning Process

- Be alert to engaging additional folks beyond those initially identified—this may seem open ended, but it is far better to bring people and groups into the formal process than it is to have to defend the process against charges of exclusivity.
- Meet with individuals and small groups to gather information and discuss needs and concepts that are developing.
- Present to mid-size and large groups to exchange ideas and get feedback on findings and proposals. This cross-talk stimulates the sense of shared responsibility as individuals and groups with different concerns come together to hear the whole range of needs expressed through the process and wrestle with the sometimes tricky balance of addressing as many of the needs as possible in a plan focused on 10-15 years.
- Distribute presentation materials to these groups for review. This can help them become more familiar with the content, or

to support thoughtful review post presentation.

At the End of the Planning Process

- Publish report(s) and insure that they are easily available in print form or on-line.
- Make presentation(s) to key groups.
- Follow up with participants making data and graphic files available so that they can be used in subsequent internal planning.
- Brief groups to discuss plan implementation progress.

An engaged community facilitates plan implementation, as more people are aware of the plan, its rationale and recommendations. The unexpected key to managing expectations is true participation.

* * *

"Where There is NO VISION, The PEOPLE PERISH" Proverbs 21:18 ~ Arthur J. Lidsky, 2009

It is not often that a quote from the Old Testament can be found in a piece about campus planning. Having an institutional vision is one of the most important first steps of a campus planning process. Yet, often it is either missing entirely or done so poorly that it squanders its impact.

Most vision statements are less about defining a future, than describing the present. They are more a mission statement that describes what the institution is presently doing than a statement of what the institution intends to become.

Most vision statements are so generic that they are interchangeable

—just swap the name of your college or university with some other institution's vision statement and see if it applies.

Words such as " we will become ..," or "we aspire to be ..," or "we will be ..," are indicative of a vision statement that is describing a future state. Jim Barker, the President of Clemson University in South Carolina had a simple but very effective vision: "Clemson will be one of the Nation's top-20 public universities." That vision has helped to transform the University.

A vision statement is worthless, if there isn't a plan to achieve it. For instance, Clemson's vision was accompanied by 27 goals that were divided into five categories: academics, research and service; campus life; student performance; educational resources; and Clemson's national reputation. Responsibility for realizing the goals was assigned to actual people or the offices they held. Both vision and goals were approved by the Board.

Clemson University Campus Plan
Clemson, SC

The results of this simple vision are:

- the hiring of 320 new faculty with an emphasis on research
- greater proportion of grad students
- increasing quality of students, faculty, and staff
- significant increase in fund-raising and capital projects
- doubled sponsored research funding in three years
- increased space
- created joint University and corporate research park
- and US News ranking moved from the mid 30s to the low 20s. In spite of the recent flap over Clemson's conduct regarding US News surveys, a rise of this magnitude would not have been possible without the strong vision and tangible results.

Shirley Ann Jackson, the President of Rensselaer Polytechnic Institute, developed another example of a simple, but effective vision: "To achieve greater prominence in the 21st century as a top-tier world-class technological research university with global reach and global impact." RPI developed 150 goals to support this vision and these goals fit into six themes: resident undergraduate education; research and graduate education; education for working professionals; scientific and technological entrepreneurship; Rensselaer communities; and enabling change. Again, key leaders were charged with achieving goals. Both vision and goals were approved by the Board.

The results of Dr. Jackson's simple vision are:

- 80 new faculty
- doubled the amount of sponsored research dollars
- anonymous gift of $360 million
- new biotechnology center

- new experimental and performing arts center
- new interactive pedagogies across all curricula

The lack of an institutional vision is a failure of leadership—because it is the responsibility of the president or the executive cabinet to create a sense of direction toward a future and a detailed, strategy and accountable plan for achieving that vision.

"The planning effectiveness of a campus depends on the planning effectiveness of its presidential leadership. There is no escape from this situation." John Millett

"You got to be careful if you don't know where you're going, because you might not get there." Yogi Berra

* * *

"Puzzling Over Priorities for Campus Planning"

~ George G. Mathey, 2012

Campus planning is, on one level, a straightforward process to develop an answer to the question, "What facilities will we need to advance our mission over the next 10-20 years?" But as we think about what should be done, and the resources we may have to make these proposals reality, it becomes clearer that it's not quite so simple. We begin to ask questions like:

- What aspect(s) of our mission are most deserving of facility support?
- Since we can only do a portion of what we'd like to do in any period, which projects are essential to our continued and greater success?

- What projects do we need to do soon, and what can be deferred?

And we begin to realize that we need to frame a dialogue that will build consensus around institutional priorities.

There are a number of possibilities for determining priorities for campus planning projects.

- The President and/or Trustees could meet to declare the high level institutional view.
- The Faculty could determine its view of priorities rooted in the academic plan.
- The Advancement Office could identify those projects most likely to resonate with donors.
- Students could decide the issue by liking projects in a Facebook poll.
- City residents could choose projects that would both provide amenities to the community while avoiding friction in the neighborhood.

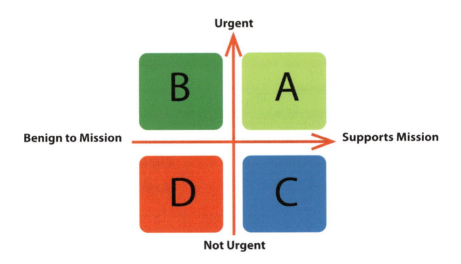

Graphic Courtesy: John Sell, College of Wooster

- The Alumni could prioritize the projects for the good of the college.
- The Consultant could dictate priorities based on his or her preferences and best professional judgment.

Perhaps all of these things could be done and then somehow synthesized to articulate the ultimate statement of institutional direction. However, this process is likely to be lengthy, potentially messy and probably somewhat divisive. What is absolutely essential about prioritization is that it is fundamentally an institutional responsibility. While consensus may be impossible, a shared vision is achievable and a strong indicator of success for plan implementation.

There are two tools we employ to get to the heart of the prioritization puzzle. The first tool is based on a simple, somewhat impressionistic matrix that responds to the ambiguity of multi-dimensional goals. Two axes bisect one another at right angles creating 4 quadrants. The vertical axis represents urgency from low to high, the horizontal axis represents alignment with mission and vision from negligible to strong. Projects are placed in each quadrant according to the project's conformance with its plotted position along both axes. We were introduced to this methodology by, John Sell, a wonderful collaborator we met in the course of our ten-year (and counting) engagement with the College of Wooster.

The second tool is a more rigorous mapping of projects and their contribution to achieving strategic goals. A matrix is developed that arrays the projects down the vertical axis and the institution's strategic goals along the horizontal axis. Each project is then assessed in regard to the impact it would have in advancing each of the goals. (a 3- or 5-point scale is sufficient). Those projects with the most points rise to the top of the priority list. An implementation plan can then be devised informed by these rankings and the logistical factors affecting project sequencing.

Clients have led us to develop other methods beyond these, but whether we use either of these methods or devise a third, the process tends to be iterative. Generally the college participants in the prioritization process should be familiar with the planning to date and in positions with at least some responsibility for implementing the plan. Basic questions participants should wrestle with prior to prioritization discussions include:

- Of this long list of projects and proposals which will most positively impact students? Why?
- Which of these initiatives best advances our core mission? How?
- How might these projects embody our vision of the future?
- If we could only do three of the things proposed, which would they be? Why?
- For each proposal, is there an acceptable (or better) way to meet the need?
- Link a project to one or more strategic goals. If you can't, does the project have a lasting justification?

Prioritization of a plan's projects and initiatives is a demanding process critical to plan success and longevity. This is the stage of the process where the excitement of developing project concepts, and receiving and assessing the possible plan alternatives gives way to reflection and hard choices from a list of attractive options. It's where the institution exerts the most influence on the development and final representation of the plan. Ensuring that a sound methodology appropriate to the culture of the institution is in place to frame this phase is a key to plan success.

* * *

"Strategic Planning and Setting Priorities"

~ Arthur J. Lidsky, 2014

A strategic plan is an essential and early first step in the campus planning process. It provides context and direction for a campus plan. Unfortunately, on many campuses, the strategic plan has lost its meaning and effectiveness. It is disconcerting to see a "strategic plan", created in a participatory process involving a broad spectrum of the community, a year or two in development, with most participants pleased with the result, formally approved, and yet—it is not a plan. Rather, it is a statement of goals. Sometimes the goals are focused on supporting the institution's mission; sometimes the goals are focused on achieving the institution's vision of the future.

Goal setting is a critically important early step in the planning process for any college or university—but goals, by themselves, do not make a plan. What is missing is the difficult piece of the process—identification of the strategies for achieving those goals and identifying the person or department who will be responsible for each strategy. See the example below from a mid-west law school's strategic plan. The school identified 6 strategic goals and 14 strategies for attaining those goals. An example of achieving one goal is described below.

Goal 2: Enhance the Experience of our Students

Strategy 1: Augment mentoring/advising, including improved curricular guidance

Strategy 2: Build on our strength in skills training

Strategy 3: Improve the first year experience

Strategy 4: Increase diversity in the student body

Strategy 5: Enhance long-term career prospects for our graduates

Action Items for Strategy 1 include:

- Improve the faculty advising program
- Hire an additional full-time academic support instructor, starting no later than FY11
- Inaugurate a "take a law professor to lunch" program, including financial support
- Increase availability of faculty for individual/small group consultation with students
- Continue to implement informal/formal gatherings with dean/associate deans to advise students/obtain feedback about student concerns
- Continue to ensure student participation on appropriate law school committees
- Continue to conduct regular meetings between deans and SBA president

In addition to having strategies for achieving those goals, the plan also had action items for realizing each strategy and a list of metrics for measuring and assessing how well the goal was being obtained.

An effective strategic plan will have the following components:

- An institutional mission and vision statement
- A set of goals
- Strategies for realizing those goals
- A time frame for the plan
- Resources required—faculty, staff, facilities, financial

- Identification of who is responsible for managing the strategies
- Priorities
- Metrics to measure progress towards strategy and action completion.

Setting Priorities

Even with a well-crafted strategic plan, an institution's physical planning will lack direction without clear decisions regarding priorities. Setting priorities ought to be fairly easy, but it is not. Each institution must decide who sets priorities and how open the process should be. Not everything is, or should be, a high priority and the process of deciding is political, emotional, social, and has implications for the curriculum, staffing, facilities, finances, and the attraction and retention of students and faculty.

There are different methods for prioritizing—from the simple grouping of projects or strategies into High, Medium, and Low categories to the same principle but different descriptor categories of Essential, Desirable, and Enhancement.

Project managers use some variation of what has become known as the Iron Triangle of Scope, Time, and Cost—sometimes using Quality instead of Scope.

There are various quantitative methods that give a semblance of rationality. Essentially, criteria are defined and each given a weighting number that represents how important that criterion might be. However, any group of committees looking at the same projects and the same criteria will inevitably differ on weights assigned and how the criteria might be applied—it is not always a replicable result.

Another method is one that Dr. Stephen Covey has described where projects or strategies are place in a matrix that has the following axis: Important—Urgent, Important—Not Urgent, Not Important—Urgent, and Not Important—Not Urgent.

The method I like is similar to Covey's and I first saw this method in use at the College of Wooster presented by Dr. John Sell. The axis of the matrix is Supports the Mission, Benign to Mission, Urgent, and Not Urgent. Those projects or strategies that fall into the quadrant of Supports Mission and Urgent would be the highest priorities while those that fall into the quadrant of Benign to Mission and Not Urgent would be the lowest priority.

The strategic plan and priorities are the essential beginning of a campus planning process. Without them, any planning process will falter and be diminished.

PART TWO

ORGANIZING FOR PLANNING

CHAPTER 2

"Good Client/Bad Client" ~ Arthur J. Lidsky, 2004

Colleges and universities hire planning consultants, architects, and other design professionals to address institutional issues and needs. In doing so, both parties enter into a legal, corporate, institutional, and personal relationship.

Whether or not the assignment is productive depends as much on the skills and experience of the consultants as on your preparedness and on the degree to which you are a responsible client.

Planning should be an on-going institutional endeavor. Bringing in a consultant to help your institution demonstrates good stewardship. However, the presence of a consultant does not eliminate your responsibilities—setting priorities, making decisions, and becoming engaged.

"The planning effectiveness of a campus depends on the planning effectiveness of its presidential leadership. There is no escape from this situation." -John Millett

As the institution's leader, you are responsible for describing the problem.

You are responsible for establishing priorities. Consultants can then help you understand the implications of your choices. Here are some useful rules-of-thumb.

If your project involves new construction, be realistic about the expenses above basic construction costs. For planning purposes, a new construction project can be 1.25 to 1.35 the cost of construction.

Be realistic about schedule. A campus plan, should take about 9 months to complete. A facility program usually requires a minimum of 3 to 4 months. New construction for an academic building will take 18 to 24 months.

If you set a challenging schedule, then you need to recognize the impact this will have on your institution. Consultants are experienced in meeting deadlines, but be sure the institution does not cause delays.

Don't be shy about being a demanding client—of your consultant and yourself. You will both be more successful.

* * *

"Who Should Be At The Table?"

~ Arthur J. Lidsky, 2004

... at the table: room at the table; a place at the table; a seat at the table; getting to the table; ...the conference table; ...the negotiating table; ...

the table of power.

The metaphor of the table, although getting old, is still a useful one for thinking about organizing a planning or design process.

Who & When

Who to involve in the process is just as important a question as when to be involved. Who and when depend on the type of project the institution is engaging in: campus plan, facility program, or architectural design.

Who also depends upon a number of other characteristics such as whether the institution is a university, college, or community college; whether it is public or private; its enrollment size; geographic location; relationship with the community; culture; organizational structure; staff availability; and financial resources.

How

Despite the nuanced differences, similarities can help structure the process and the selection of participants. Most facility-related projects require at least two committees: an executive committee as well as a user-group committee.

The executive committee should consist of the chief academic officer, the vice presidents, and, exofficio, the president. For continuity and communication, the chair of the user-group committee should also be a member of the executive committee. The make-up of the latter committee depends upon the type of project.

Campus Planning

Although a campus planning process requires community-wide participation, the user-group committee should not exceed seven to nine representatives or it becomes unwieldy and less participatory. Since the committee is intentionally small, other techniques can ensure broad institutional interaction and participation, including task forces; focus groups; workshops; and formal and informal meetings, reviews, interviews, and presentations.

A campus planning user-group committee should consist of faculty, staff, and student representatives. Committee members must have no, or appear to have no, particular agenda—and the institutional community should trust and respect them. It is useful to have several senior faculty and representation from residential life, campus life, physical plant, finance or development, staff, and student government. Some campuses might elect to have a Board member on the committee —but it is best to keep fiduciary and oversight responsibility separate.

Facility Programming & Architectural Design

Memberships of user-group committees formed for facility programming or architectural design are typically more homogeneous and specific to a particular discipline or project than committees for campus planning. Both should have no more than seven to nine members. Because of their narrow focus, the programming or architectural design committees can easily become quite parochial —concentrating on their specific discipline requirements and losing sight of the institutional context. To prevent this, include one or two representatives from other areas of the college or university. If the project is a science facility, for example, a representative from the social sciences or humanities on the committee ensures that decisions aren't made in isolation.

No matter who is chosen to sit at the table, the success of a project depends upon the care with which you set the table—the early pre-planning that must take place—selecting the participants, agreeing on assumptions, concurring on priorities, articulating a vision, and defining the process and schedule.

* * *

"The Seven C's of Choosing Consultants"
~ Arthur J. Lidsky, 2004

Cause

What is the reason for engaging a consultant? Is it to address physical, academic, organizational, or financial issues? Usually they are interrelated. The type of consultant will depend on the desired comprehensiveness of the solution.

Committee

Private institutions have more flexibility in assembling the committee than do public colleges and universities. Nonetheless, those that will be affected by the study should have strong representation in the selection of the consultant! A committee of seven to nine members is ideal. The user committee, the committee that interacts with the consultant during the course of the study should be different from the selection committee.

Cadence

Make sure that you and the consultant have a realistic schedule for institutional review, collegial discussion, consensus building, fund raising, and design and construction if that is a solution. The success of your project depends, to a large part, on the character and quality of discussion, communication, and consensus.

Conflict

All major issues related to curriculum, number of students, faculty, and staff, mode of teaching, organization, and priorities should be resolved prior to choosing an architectural consultant.

Cost

Be careful of the low bid and limited scope which then expands during the reality of the study and every minor change becomes an add-on. If there is a budget target on a construction project, make sure that the consultant understands that the target is the PROJECT cost and includes the cost of construction as well as such costs as: A/E fees, furnishing and equipment, contingencies, and administration costs.

Communication

This is your responsibility—you must articulate exactly what you really would like the consultant to do. Preparing a concise and accurate RFP or RFQ is critical to the choice of consultant and success of the project.

Compatibility

The mystic magic of compatibility—of chemistry—of choosing a consultant with the right personality for your campus's particular circumstance and the unique personalities of the people who will work together for a long and intense time.

* * *

"The Project Shepherd" ~ Arthur J. Lidsky, 2009

Shepherd (n) O.E. sceaphierde, from sceap "sheep" + hierde "herder," from heord "a herd" (see herd). Cf. M.L.G., M.Du. schaphirde, M.H.G. schafhirte, Ger. dial. schafhirt. Shepherds customarily were buried with a tuft of wool in hand, to prove their occupation on Doomsday and be excused for often missing Sunday church. The metaphoric verbal sense of "watch over or guide" is first recorded 1820. Shepherd's pie is recorded from 1877. (etymonline.com)

The term "project shepherd" has become widely used in the planning and programming of science facilities—championed by Project Kaleidoscope (PKAL), a major force in science facilities and curriculum planning and design. It was first used by Dot Widmayer, a biologist at Wellesley College, now retired. She defined her role as three-fold: first and foremost, it was to protect the space program that the College created through a participatory process that engaged departments, faculty, staff, and students. Secondly, it was to provide institutional memory from the beginning of the planning and programming process through architectural design, and through construction. Lastly, it was to provide open communication throughout the long, complex process of defining, designing, and constructing a science building. It was to make sure that key College people were at the table whenever a decision was being made that had any impact on the program.

The role of shepherd or project coordinator is absolutely essential on all college and university renovation and new construction projects. Often, it falls on the shoulders of someone from Facilities. Sometimes a college or university administrator, either academic or financial, volunteers to play this role. In my mind for any projects impacting academic facilities, it should be someone from the academic arena. Facilities must be at the table, but not as the shepherd.

The project shepherd should be fair and evenhanded and have the trust of the faculty. The shepherd should have no particular agenda other than advancement of the goals of the project. To be effective, the shepherd will need some form of release time for the duration of the project: probably 2 to 3 years. Furthermore, if the shepherd is a faculty member, then being tenured is important, as serving in this role will divert time from the work and experiences critical to those seeking tenure.

✳ ✳ ✳

"Good Teams" ~ George G. Mathey, 2010

Erika's piece (see page 158) on public-private housing partnerships stresses the critical importance of the project team to ensure the good communication that leads to a high-quality outcome.

Over the years, many institutions have increasingly preferred planning project teams composed of multiple firms to ensure maximum coverage of all systems from academic to waste water.

These large teams require strong leadership. The team's lead firm must have deep experience in-house and good team management and coordination skills.

Applying all team members' talents to the project in appropriate amounts at the right time requires clarity about desired outcomes as a key starting point. While the project team can help identify, refine and articulate the scope and depth of deliverables, this is fundamentally a client responsibility, so spend some time during the drafting of the RFP focusing on the specifics of the deliverables. After all, these are the tangible products that will represent the many hours of work and collaboratively-generated wisdom of the project team. The documents will be used over several years to guide decisions on campus development. Talk with your colleagues about what your institution requires of these products? Who will use them? How will you use them? Answers to these questions early in the project will guarantee a satisfactory outcome.

When evaluating teams, consider combining local expertise with national (or even international) experience. Teams that meld these perspectives and knowledge will provide stronger input and richer solutions.

If yours is a large, complex institution, a large, complex team may well be necessary. For smaller colleges and universities, a small team is beautiful. If specialized assessments and knowledge are required, these skills can be added to the team as needed in a focused way, rather than bloating the team (and its fees) from project inception to completion.

Finally, in team selection, pay attention to the personality and character of the team leader. Campus plans typically take several months to complete, and the quality of the relationship with this person can make the difference between an adequate and an excellent plan.

PART THREE

CAMPUS PLANNING

CHAPTER 3

"A Perspective on Campus Planning"

~ Arthur J. Lidsky

Everyday, college and university campuses change—usually imperceptibly and occasionally dramatically. Programs change, people change, financial resources change, buildings change, land and landscapes change, environs change. The way our campuses look today is the result of all the minor and significant, casual and formal, rational and irrational decisions that are made in the day-to-day dynamic interaction of a living institution responding to such changes. The impetus for new construction of college and university buildings in the 1950's and '60s was increasing enrollments and expanding programs. Today, the forces for change on campuses are a myriad of complex issues—for example:

- Changes in the academic disciplines
- An increase in and awareness of interrelated disciplines

- Decreased federal and state funds for programs, operations, research, and facilities
- Increasing awareness of environmental issues and concerns—"green architecture" and campus design;
- Increasing competition of for-profit institutions and on-line programs
- An increasing interrelationship between business, industry, and educational institutions
- Increasing numbers of faculty and students (including undergraduates) involved in research at both the university and college level
- Increasing federal and state regulations and standards for life safety and building safety
- Increasing use and sophistication of instrumentation, computers, and various presentation and communication media
- Pedagogical changes such as an increasing effort to involve students in the process of learning by doing—experiential learning
- Student consumer shopping for the college of his or her choice
- The ticking time bomb of deferred maintenance

Given all these forces, colleges and universities must plan deliberately, carefully, and rationally. Planning must become a fundamental and underlying theme woven tightly into the day-to-day operations and interactions of the institution, whatever its type. The future health of higher education depends upon better planning and management. The planning process described in Figure 12.1 is necessarily generic but can be tailored and shaped to fit the needs and circumstances of all.

Campus planning is the process of identifying and guiding those institutional decisions in higher education that have spatial implications. The responsibility of academic leaders, it is a process of guiding the development of a campus so that it supports functional, aesthetic, and economic goals within the context of an institution's history, mission, and vision for the future.

There are today over four thousand (4,000) colleges and universities in America; they differ by mission, by academic objectives, and by program emphasis. Enrollments range in size from several hundred students to more than 50,000 students. The institutions differ from the perspective of numbers of faculty and staff; resources fiscal and physical, including levels of endowment; and forms of governance. And today we must add the for-profit category to this taxonomy.

However, higher education is more complex than that simple differentiation of public, private, and for-profit suggests. The taxonomy can be expanded to include residential and commuter and institutions with national, regional, and local focus. Even that taxonomy is too general, for institutions can be further described as urban, suburban, or rural; a city college, state university, land- or sea-grant institution, research university, liberal arts college, or community college. The definitions can be expanded to include coed, male, female, religious, military, and historically black. Some can be further refined, for example, by subject: business, law, or engineering.

Conceptually, the campus planning process can be divided into different components that are addressed sequentially, iteratively, or concurrently. (Figure 12.1). Although these steps for planning are generic and can be used in a variety of contexts, for institutions seeking

Figure 12.1: Campus Planning Process

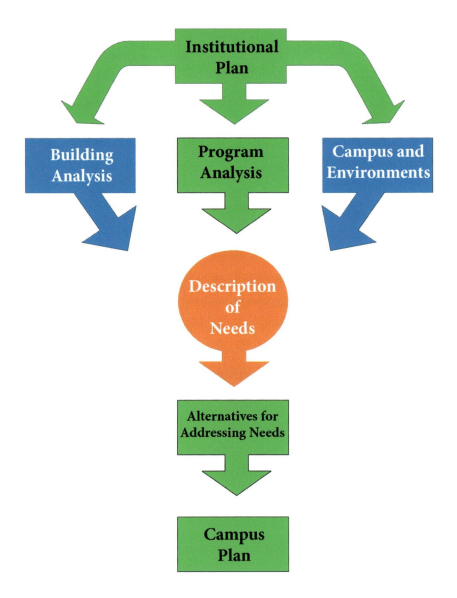

to build and sustain strong undergraduate programs in mathematics and the various fields of science, this comprehensive planning process is crucial. Maintaining strong programs in these fields is a costly endeavor, over the short as well as the long terms. Institutional leaders, who must make decisions about using resources prudently and creatively, have to decide at every step about the cost of decisions made and those not made. For the number of students involved, the costs of maintaining strength in these STEM fields may appear disproportionate, particularly in comparison to other departments with higher enrollments. However, as science and technology have an increasing impact on all life and work, colleges and universities, and those leading them have a responsibility to make a rigorous encounter with these fields an integral part of the undergraduate curriculum for all students.

The advice that follows outlines considerations for trustees, presidents and other academic leaders in early stages in considering making a major investment in facilities that support learning, teaching, and research in mathematics, technology and the various fields of science and engineering.

Institutional Plan

There are five interrelated elements of the institutional plan: mission statement, academic plan, staffing plan, capital budget plan, and the operating budget plan. Of the five, the academic plan is the most central, but without a solid statement of mission in place that outlines a vision of the institutional future, there should be no final decisions made about the academic plan. This is because there must be a campus-wide understanding about how building and sustaining strong programs in science and mathematics connect to the institutional mission. However, once academic planning is underway and guided by the mission statement, it becomes the pivotal element.

An academic plan should have a point of view about programs and curriculum, about enrollments and staffing, and about programs that will grow, remain constant, be reduced or eliminated, or nurtured as special resources. All other institutional planning will flow from the goals, objectives, and priorities of the academic plan. On many campuses, building consensus and reaching closure during the academic planning process will take several years.

Building, Program, and Campus and Environs Analysis

Following or coincident with institutional planning is an institutional audit of the physical infrastructure: an assessment of the existing buildings, campus, infrastructure, and environs. Here generic questions about spaces and the physical infrastructure need to be asked:

- How much space does the institution have to support its mission and academic plan, today and into the future?
- Are the amount, condition, configuration, and use of space appropriate?
- Are the spaces sufficiently flexible to support programmatic change over time?
- Are the buildings capable of sustaining network, media, and communications improvements?
- What are the critical spatial relationships, patterns of interactions?

This analysis of campus and environs usually consists of some combination of an assessment of building location and use, land ownership, open space and landscape, pedestrian and vehicular circulation, parking, topography, and utility infrastructure. In some instances, a detailed infrastructure analysis is conducted prior to or as a separate part of the campus planning study.

The analysis then moves to an assessment of the academic programs relative to campus resources in terms of the degree to which those spaces and environs support current and planned changes in learning, teaching and research. In the context of making decisions about serving a mission and academic plan that focuses on strengthening student learning in fields of mathematics, science, engineering, and technology, questions such as the following need to be asked:

- How many faculty, students, and staff are there today, and how many will there be tomorrow?
- What is the level of research activity expected of those faculty and of the engagement of undergraduates in that faculty research?
- What is the nature of each department's pedagogy, what new approaches are being considered?
- What will be in the impact of technologies in undergraduate learning?
- How will the pedagogy change, and do the physical resources help or hinder the program?
- What are the critical programmatic affinities?
- Are new interdisciplinary programs anticipated?
- Is there to be an increase of students engaged in learning these fields?

Description of Needs

The goal of this analysis of facilities, program, and campus is to provide a foundation for developing a description of precise facilities needs required to support the mission and academic plan. Needs may vary from minor staffing requirements or cosmetic changes, to improvements that may involve renovating or adding to an existing building, to the construction of an entirely new building. Campuses with different missions and identities will arrive at a distinctly different set of needs, but at institutions of all types the grounding question for this analysis should be, what difference will this make to our efforts to strengthen student learning?

Developing this list of needs, like attending to the mission statement, must be through a participatory process involving a broad spectrum of the community. A key objective here is consensus; however, the list of needs must not be a wish list reflecting individual wants and desires. Comparisons with peers, the use of standard guidelines, and the application of best practices can play a role in keeping the what are viewed as needs in line with reality. (This is a point at which academic leaders must be certain that they and their faculty colleagues are connected to colleagues beyond their campus, aware of the achievements of others pursuing similar educational and institutional goals.) Each item must be carefully vetted and justified in the context of the institutional mission and the consensus in regard to the academic plan. Finally, agreement should be arrived at in regard to priorities from that list, and this agreement document should be publicized widely. This is particular important in considering the major financial investments that are probable if new spaces for science are to take shape. The entire campus community must buy into the need, and this will only happen as they are convinced that addressing these needs serve the larger institutional mission and goals.

Alternatives for Addressing Needs

Once there is agreement on needs and priorities, campus leaders can explore alternatives for addressing the needs. Some alternatives might be operational: a change in the way in which rooms are scheduled, for instance; or the sharing of sophisticated instrumentation and equipment. Other alternatives may relate to the physical infrastructure, with little visible impact on the campus, while others may have significant impact on open space, circulation, aesthetics, and the campus as a whole. If this becomes the option, leaders will have to make decisions that address the domino effect that happens on a campus when a major improvement or new construction is considered.

Facility alternatives can vary in scale; they can be some combination of reallocated space and relocated functions requiring minor renovation, to significant renovation, the construction of new space added to a building, or the construction of a new building. If a building has historic significance, restoration could be a major factor. Short-term solutions to nagging problems may surface at this stage, and leaders must be alert to this. Arriving at new spaces is, ultimately an extended process, and some needs (student gathering spaces, more technological connections, classrooms with chairs on wheels) can be addressed quickly and at modest cost.

For many, this stage of the planning process is the most enjoyable and most exciting. New ideas and possibilities are explored. Large portions of the institution's community come together in small and large groups to discuss possibilities. The possibilities seem endless, but they are not. Just as the preparation of the list of needs should be done to avoid a wish list, alternatives should be categorized by the degree of feasibility and necessity. The difficult part of this phase of the planning process is the selection of criteria against which the alternatives will be measured and judged. Criteria could include factors relating to construction, project, and operating costs; timing and phasing; the extent to which the alternative meets programmatic requirements; the extent to which the alternative meets specified spatial relationships and design goals; the extent to which the siting of a new building enhances the overall campus design; and so on.

An important reason to give serious attention to a wide range of alternatives is that as the project proceeds, unanticipated difficulties and opportunities will surface (for example, not enough funds, an unexpected gift, a new faculty appointment with research interests not served in planning). By having a wide range of alternatives already on the table, you will be better prepared to keep the project on schedule.

The Campus Plan

Once the assessment of alternatives is complete, emerging from a broad-based, widely-participatory process, a campus plan begins to take shape. Often during this process, new alternatives have risen and others begin to connect in new ways. Finally, through fiat or consensus, one set of alternatives is chosen to address the defined needs and priorities. This then becomes the campus plan.

Since implementing all the elements of the campus plan at once is usually impossible, campus leaders must set priorities to accomplish projects over a defined time period, say, ten to fifteen years. Most campuses reevaluate projects—and their costs and benefits—after five to seven years. Based on the needs and assumptions at that time, the plan is either confirmed or modified to reflect current realities.

Campus plans are usually summarized with graphics and text. Often the audience is both internal and external. For the college or university community, the plan is a record of the process, analysis, needs, alternatives considered, and the plan itself. External audiences can be state offices responsible for funding or other governance entities, as well as potential donors.

The planning documentation will include sections on context and background, a description of the existing situation, a description of the analysis of current building and campus, an outline of programmatic initiatives and needs based on the institutional plan. There will also be a visual presentation of the campus plan, with a birds-eye view to illustrate the intention; there will be preliminary determinations about phasing and implementing the plan, along with the estimates of costs to be associated with each stage.

Conclusion

Planning gives your institution an opportunity to ask fundamental questions about mission, program, fiscal resources, facilities, and environs. To be effective, planning must be participatory and involve those who will be affected by the plan: students, faculty, staff, and the community. Planning becomes the framework for addressing those questions in an integrated, open, and rational process.

A campus ultimately is an expression of its mission and educational philosophy. It reveals understandings about the relationship between how and what and where students learn. Those of us involved in this aspect of Project Kaleidoscope over the past decade have come to see how the planning of new spaces and structures for science can be a defining moment in the life of the institution. In this planning, decisions are made that give evidence of how a particular college and university is responding to the contextual changes: serving all students, infusing the learning environment with the excitement of discovery, and accommodating new directions in science.

References:

Keller, G. *Academic Strategy*, Baltimore, Md.: Johns Hopkins University Press, 1983. Millett, J. "Relating Governance to Leadership." In P. Jedamus and M.W. Peterson (eds.), *Improving Academic Management: Handbook for Planning and Institutional Research*. San Francisco: JOSSEY-BASS, 1980

Source:

New Directions for Higher Education, no. 119, Fall 2002,
JOSSEY-BASS

* * *

"When Not to Initiate A Campus Plan"
(if you can avoid it and what to do when
you can't) ~ George G. Mathey, 2004

The most productive campus plans are organic processes that require stable, sure leadership; an inspiring vision of the institution's future; accurate, current information; and meaningful, timely engagement by an active campus community.

When you lack an internal advocate for the outcomes

This is the most crucial requirement. Without a respected, authoritative internal point person, any plan process is likely to falter at some stage. It must be obvious to the leadership team on campus who this person will be before starting a plan. If, for reasons of institutional culture or politics, the president will not be the lead person, it is the president's responsibility to identify, cultivate, encourage, and support the best person for this role.

Institutional planning is a continuous activity at well-managed campuses. Having the right person leading the effort is essential to producing meaningful, vibrant, successful plans, and eliminates the possibility of its becoming a going-through-the-motions routine.

When changing administrations

Campus planning processes benefit from strong leadership at the highest levels. When a president or a vice-president involved in a plan suddenly moves on or is due to retire, it can have a crippling effect on plan process and quality. People are often too unsure of the new administration's direction to participate confidently. The re-ordered priorities of the incoming leadership can reconfigure academic, student life and administrative initiatives championed by the outgoing administration, creating a difficult environment for planning.

If this happens, design the process to go into hiatus when the campus and program analysis is complete and initial plan concepts have been drafted. The incoming administration can then get settled and take the leadership of the development of plan alternatives.

When you have a micro-managing board

While an institution's board must have solid connections with campus planning processes, hands-on direction from an overly enthusiastic individual will not result in excellent planning, no matter how well intentioned the person may be.

Effective campus planning is an administrative responsibility that the board needs to participate in, but should not direct.

Before you have agreement on enrollment projections or enrollment scenarios

Without a holistic understanding of enrollment goals and a strategy for achieving them, the campus plan's attempts to accommodate future needs become mere conjecture. Have an enrollment plan in place early so it dovetails with the physical planning.

When you don't have adequate documentation of your physical assets

This seems obvious, but it is not fully in place at many institutions. This documentation is essential to the integrity of planning efforts. You can't manage what you don't understand. If materials such as an up-to-date campus map and building floor plans, a room-by-room facility inventory, and building condition assessments do not exist in useful formats at the outset of a plan, then include them as a part of the effort and appropriate funds to this fundamental data generation.

* * *

"Campus Design and Campus Planning – Don't Confuse Them" ~ Arthur J. Lidsky, 2004

Campus planning is a broad and inclusive decision making process. The campus *plan* is a product of that process while campus *design* is an intrinsic characteristic of the campus plan.

Difficulties arise when one is confused with the other. Design without comprehensive planning is *ad hoc* and lacks substance. Often, a college or university seeks a campus plan, but develops a campus design, without understanding the difference, and without understanding or appreciating the complexity of the planning process.

Vocabulary Distinguishes Planning from Design Key

The vocabulary that is used with planning and design is different as well. In planning, discussions focus on mission, vision, needs, programs, initiatives, curriculum, pedagogy, research, alternatives, benchmarking, condition, consensus, enrollment, funding, implementation, interaction, participation, peer comparison, timeframe, and utilization.

Words and concepts used in the process of campus design include: architectural style, building elements, campus style, design principles, campus characteristics, landscape, lighting, materials, massing, natural site characteristics, outdoor spaces, pedestrian circulation, scale, signage, street furniture, topography, and vehicular circulation.

Successful Campus Planning Begins with the Institution's Mission and Vision

To be successful, campus planning should encompass broad representation and participation within the institution and be intricately intertwined with the college or university's strategic, academic, and enrollment plans, campus life initiatives, and financial resources. The beginning point, of course, must be the institution's mission and vision.

John Carroll University recently developed one of the best examples of mission and vision incorporated into the planning process. Although used primarily for facility planning, it is a model for campus planning as well. Fundamental to the vision were six themes: curriculum integration, use of technology, student recruitment and retention, student and faculty research, pedagogy and faculty/student relationships, and pre-k-12 science and mathematics education. Each theme had its rationale, set of goals, and implementation strategies for realizing the goals. Some of the strategies had staffing implications, others had campus and facility implications, and still others had programmatic or pedagogical consequences.

Successful Campus Design Has a Set of Guiding Assumptions

Campus design, like campus planning, should have an underlying and guiding set of assumptions. Without institutional agreement on a campus design philosophy, design of a campus will be based on the architectural fad du jour, or the loudest voice, or a donor's desires.

In preparing design guidelines for future campus development, Clemson University identified overarching design principles. These principles fall into three categories—to promote intellectual and social interaction, to respect cultural and historic resources, and to value sustainable design. From these principles, Clemson developed a set of design guidelines and planning standards that provide the University with a working framework to guide any changes to the campus. The design guidelines are more specific than the principles and provide direction for campus design, landscape, and building projects.

Campus planning and campus design—process and product; both rely on fundamental but different assumptions; both require a related but different approach. Planning is action oriented—design shapes the action. Don't confuse the two.

* * *

"The Death of the Campus Master Plan"

~ Arthur J. Lidsky, 2005

At one time, the term "Master Plan" had a meaning that all who used it seemed to understand. Today, it has lost that meaning: it seems as if any planning or design is a "Master Plan."

It reminds me of the word "love" which used to have a specific meaning and now is used casually to mean anything from copulation, to affection, to like, to zero in tennis.

Most colleges and universities use the term master plan with little understanding or differentiation.

Architects are notorious for using the term "master" for almost any project—all plans, or rather designs, are "master plans." In addition to campus master plans, I have seen master plans for a section of a campus, and master plans for individual buildings. I have seen master plans for windows and master plans for toilets. What does the word "master" mean in any of these contexts? Whatever you wish —and therefore it means little—and, in fact, the use of the term adds a level of implied importance and thoroughness that is misleading. Institutions are making multimillion dollar decisions based on incomplete information and information that is out of context with the broad picture.

I once saw a university that had a science building master plan, and a master plan for a group of science buildings, and a master plan for the campus. Of course, each of these master plans had little in common.

The term master plan used to mean the predominant plan under which all other plans conform. It was meant to be the predominant plan that would give guidance and create the context for other, dependent plans, and subsequent design.

It is no longer a useful term to describe the complex, comprehensive, participatory process that integrates academic, financial, and facility planning. There are several professional planning organizations that stress the need for integrated planning. The Society for College and University Planning (SCUP) and Project Kaleidoscope (PKAL) are two examples. Both stress the need for mission, vision, and academic plan to be the driving force for campus planning. Both stress the need to integrate academics, finances, and facilities. Despite their efforts, most campus "master" plans lack an in-depth, inclusive, comprehensive planning process.

I would like us to drop the meaningless term master plan and use some other term to reflect what a master plan should actually be—integrated and comprehensive. The essential characteristics of a campus plan should be the integration of academic, financial, campus life, and facility issues. So in that regard, I vote for integrated campus planning.

Why is this important? Because the quality of campus planning has declined as the meaning of the term "master" has become diluted. As less emphasis is placed on the need to integrate academic and financial planning with physical planning, the so-called master plan has become merely a physical design.

Love, Arthur

* * *

"The Learning Campus and Campus Planning"
~ Arthur J. Lidsky, 2005

Terry O'Banion, in his book, A Learning College for the 21st Century, said "The learning college places learning first and provides educational experiences for learners anyway, anyplace, anytime." Although the term "learning college" has its basis in the community college environment, the concept (or at least the term) has spread to 4-year and graduate institutions as well.

The learning campus shifts the "teachable moment" to the learning moment—"anyway, anyplace, any time." The shift is from faculty giving and student taking to student doing.

Another shift in the learning campus is the understanding that all members of the institution are learners: students, faculty, staff, and administrators—a true community of learners.

What are the spatial implications of "anyway, anyplace, anytime" and what are the implications for campus planning?

The "learning campus" requires a fundamental change in the way that the college or university community interact, not just in the classroom, but also everywhere on campus and in every endeavor.

For one thing, a "learning campus" means that the classroom and lab are not and should not be the only places where learning takes place. Offices, lounges, dorm rooms, corridors, outdoor spaces, and the myriad formal and informal gathering spaces are all important to the learning experience.

For another, it means supporting the reality that people learn at different rates, with different tools, in different settings, with the need for introspection, and the need for interaction—learning is private and independent and learning is social and dependent. A campus needs spaces, inside and out, that recognize and encourage the diversity of learning styles and approaches.

And for yet another, it means that there should be programs and places for faculty, staff, and administrators to work independently and in groups—to learn, to experiment, to assess what works, and to grow. An example of such programs is the Reflective Practice initiative at the University of New Hampshire, which encourages faculty to step back and assess what works, to work collaboratively, and to change the way faculty interact with their students.

In reflecting the "learning campus" the campus plan would include additional outdoor seating areas placed along well-traveled pedestrian routes; café options perhaps in the library or the prime athletic/recreation building; large faculty offices that would be an alternate venue for learning; small group collaboration spaces; studies and lounges of various sizes in the library and in other campus buildings, and space that would encourage interdisciplinary learning through centers and institutes or through facilitating interaction among academic departments.

The campus planning process itself should be a learning experience for the whole campus. What does planning actually mean? How do you build consensus? How do you set priorities? How do you create a vision for the future? How do you create an environment where all voices are heard and valued? What information is important? What are our values? The opportunities for learning are enormous—and the more you invite and involve faculty, staff, students, and administrators in the process, the greater the learning.

And it should be a learning experience for the consultant as well. We learn by listening, by understanding, and by learning the values and culture of an institution. The worst consultant is the one who comes to campus with the answers, with the solution, with the template, with the plan.

* * *

"The Teaching Campus: The Unstated Messages" ~ Michael Flusche, 2005
(former Associate Vice Chancellor of Syracuse University)

Colleges and universities communicate with the public in many ways: most obviously in the classroom, but also, for example, through the person of the chancellor or president, printed brochures, alumni magazines, news releases, and through high school college fairs. Those public relations and marketing avenues are usually carefully attended to.

Sometimes, however, the most important communication medium is not so carefully addressed: the campus itself. The physical environment of the campus is one of the most powerful communication channels available to an institution. Students, staff and faculty members spend many hours every week reading between the lines of the campus they inhabit. The campus's message also reaches alumni and the public at large and most especially potential students and their parents. (It is well established that the campus visit is one of the most important elements in determining students' choice of colleges.)

A careful study of what subliminal messages a campus actually sends can suggest ways a college or university can clarify or reinforce its messages to its many audiences, most especially to its students. It can be difficult for people who work at a college every day to see it with fresh eyes, to read the messages that the campus is sending, what lessons it is teaching. Therefore special efforts are often needed to see the campus afresh.

Here are some sample starter questions that can trigger an investigation of what messages the campus is sending or what lessons it is teaching:

Is the physical environment welcoming?

Are the needs of visitors well attended to: is visitor parking clearly marked? Are signage and wayfinding aids convenient, visible, and helpful? Are pathways clean, safe, and well lit? Are members of minority populations made welcome through statues, pictures, and other symbols of inclusion? Do "blue lights" and other security devices and policies reflect serious attention to student safety?

Who does the institution celebrate?

Besides the common donors plaques, are exemplary works by students and faculty celebrated and easily seen on campus? Are student art works, demonstration projects, or research papers readily available in the student center, library, or in building entranceways? Is faculty work easily found-their publications, inventions, or personal hobbies? Are notable alumni visibly held up as role models for future generations through Walls of Honor or other ongoing modes of recognition?

What values are proclaimed?

Is the college motto or inscription of the seal integrated in decorative schemes? Are there monuments, statues, or portraits celebrating civic virtue or notable contributions by members of the college community? Are student codes of conduct or expected behaviors posted in residence halls or other locations? If it is a religious institution, are appropriate symbols and images clearly evident? Are there sites on campus that celebrate the institution's history and heritage?

Is student learning the most prominent value of the institution? Are the classrooms, laboratories, studios, and library the best maintained, equipped, and comfortable spaces on campus? Do campus policies such as quiet hours and the provision of study spaces encourage serious academic work? Do academic departments welcome students and facilitate faculty-student contact? Do offices post pictures of members of the faculty, staff, and administration so that students will recognize them by sight?

What behaviors are encouraged?
Do entrances to academic buildings convey what transpires inside and entice passersby to come inside? Do the locations and arrangements of casual seating encourage both quiet personal retreats and social interactions among students? Are attractive trash receptacles conveniently placed to discourage littering?

How "green" is the campus?
Does the campus teach environmental sustainability by its policies and its promotion of ecologically sound practices in building design and fixtures? Is landscaping sensitive to the local climate and soil condition? Are there posted reminders of good practice such as turning out the lights in unoccupied rooms?

These questions, and others more specific to an institution may suggest opportunities to make the physical environment more supportive of the educational mission of the college or university.

* * *

"An Optimal Planning Approach"
~ George G. Mathey, 2006

Campus and facility planning taken together form a distinct discipline founded on a definite approach that borrows from some related disciplines (e.g., architectural and landscape design) and overlaps with others (e.g., academic/strategic planning, and educational theory).

Each of these "donor" disciplines has its own strengths. Each is required at certain stages of the campus development process. The strength of properly executed campus planning is the synthesis of disciplines, enabling institutions to create the uniquely proper campus.

In twenty years of practice, the truest of the truisms I have encountered is that each campus is different and distinct.

While superficially this comes across as an insipid, self-congratulatory statement, its truth can be demonstrated by example. Try to think of two campuses that are alike in all aspects—I firmly believe it is impossible.

Even institutions of similar size, mission, age, region, and resources will be unique and distinctive. History, founding impulse, neighboring land uses, and, most importantly, people guarantee distinctiveness.

The genius of integrated campus planning is that it enables a campus's stewards to ensure, enhance, and optimize campus distinction to advance institutional goals in the most supportive way. None of the other disciplines alone can produce the same results.

Dick Dober's pithy diagram from 1964's *Campus Planning*

illustrates the issue. Planning begins with an institution's mission, vision, academic/strategic plan, history, aspirations and people here identified by the *Program* block. Campus *Design* skills are brought to the process to respond to *Program* needs.

Where the two disciplines overlap and interact is where *Planning* thrives. I've overlaid the element of *Finance* to reinforce the idea that an institution's plans need to be guided and informed by its financial planning to maintain relevance and support implementation.

Campus Planning is at once analytical and creative, process—driven and inspiration-guided. Thoughtfully integrated planning recognizes the centrality of mission and program, while realizing the essential contributions of meaningful design thinking responding to the constraints of the built environment.

The diagram suggests the inclusiveness required for developing solid, implementable plans that derive support from an institution's many constituencies. Weaving these three planning strands together

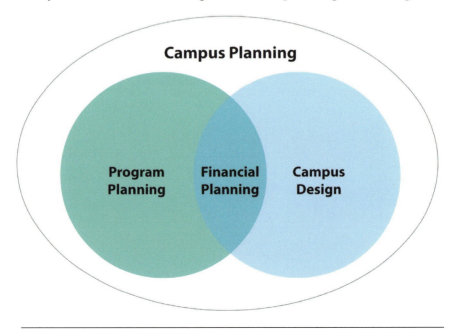

into a process that is itself a key outcome of the planning demands specific skills and a well-defined approach that can only be acquired through practice.

Educational institutions should be aware of the critical distinctiveness of this process and the skills, approaches, attitudes, and interests needed to translate its goals into a vision of its future campus.

Just as building design benefits from a preceding phase of facility programming that focuses attention on identifying, rationalizing, quantifying and describing the occupants' functional needs, campus development is greatly enhanced by periodic campus planning that focuses on institutional direction, strategic goals and campus-wide dynamics that no amount of project planning and design alone can achieve.

* * *

"Planning and Design"~ George G. Mathey, 2010

As campus and facility planners, we often describe our work as pre-architectural. That is, we work to help our clients make decisions about mission- and vision-driven campus development, renovation and new construction. This activity is an essential step for orderly, effective campus renewal and growth and is an important precursor to architectural design—the development of concepts, drawings and specifications for construction of a new building.

So while our work is pre-architectural, it encompasses both planning and design.

Some definitions can be helpful:

planning noun

The act or process of making or carrying out plans; specifically: the establishment of goals, policies, and procedures for a social or economic unit <city planning> <business planning>

-merriam-webster.com

A set of intended actions, through which one expects to achieve a goal.

-wiktionary.org

Planning in organizations and public policy is both the organizational process of creating and maintaining a plan; and the psychological process of thinking about the activities required to create a desired goal on some scale. As such, it is a fundamental property of intelligent behavior. This thought process is essential to the creation and refinement of a plan, or integration of it with other plans, that is, it combines forecasting of developments with the preparation of scenarios of how to react to them. An important, albeit often ignored aspect of planning, is the relationship it holds with forecasting. Forecasting can be described as predicting what the future will look like, whereas planning predicts what the future should look like.   -wikipedia.org

design *noun*

1. *A plan (with more or less detail) for the structure and functions of an artifact, building or system.*
2. *A pattern, as an element of a work of art or architecture.*
3. *The composition of a work of art.*
4. *Intention or plot.*
5. *The shape or appearance given to an object, especially one that is intended to make it more attractive.*
6. *The art of designing*   -Wiktionary

Planning and design are different but similar, like fraternal twins.

It is revealing that in the examples above design is often defined as dependent on planning.

Any good design has benefitted from the planning (however unconscious) that supports its execution.

Any good plan has benefitted from its intrinsic design and from designs that illustrate the plan.

Planning tends to the Apollonian, design tends to the Dionysian.

Planning is more aligned with craft while design is more aligned with art.

For individuals, planning can be spontaneous and nearly indistinguishable from design.

For complex organizations, formal planning is an essential foundation for design. The discipline, inclusiveness, analysis, prediction and order of planning informs campus design making it stronger and more integrated with institutional goals and vision.

We believe that serious planning is often overlooked or short-circuited by the excitement generated by a compelling design. For this reason, our approach to campus planning is to emphasize the planning process to ensure for our clients a solid basis for decision-making that is sensitive to change and can inspire multiple design solutions— executed by us or the many other talented designers at work today.

The quote below comes from a talk I heard 26 years ago given by John Whiteman, a former urban planning faculty member at the Harvard Graduate School of Design. I believe he credited someone else but I have been unable to track down the original source.

Do you want to influence the shape and character of a campus, neighborhood, city or nation, or would you rather decide the precise location of a window mullion?   -Anon.

This question summarizes how I feel about the relationship between planning and design and helps crystallize for me the importance of the planning activity and its benefits for colleges and universities.

Planning & Design Graphics

The differences between the planning and design stages are perhaps most tellingly revealed by the ways we illustrate our thoughts at each stage. Planning graphics tend to be simple, germinal, suggestive, and in a very intentional way, not quite complete. The goal is to convey information and, hopefully a bit of spirit, but to leave room for multiple interpretations.

Design graphics in architecture, at least, can range from the loosely pictorial to the nearly photographic as the concept evolves into a design and then the detailed instructions for building.

Below are two drawing sequences that start with planning diagrams we prepared in our initial studies for the projects followed by drawings by the talented architects that were subsequently commissioned to translate the planning into exemplary building and campus environments.

The first of these illustrates an addition to the Thayer School of Engineering at Dartmouth College.

The second maps (on page 70) the development sequence from programming, through campus planning and building design. Our thanks and respects to the architects for the use of their drawings in this illustration of planning & design graphics.

Thayer School of Engineering
Dartmouth College
Hanover, NH

DLM Concept Site Diagram 2000

Koetter Kim Rendering 2004

Completed - MacLean Engineering
Sciences Center 2006

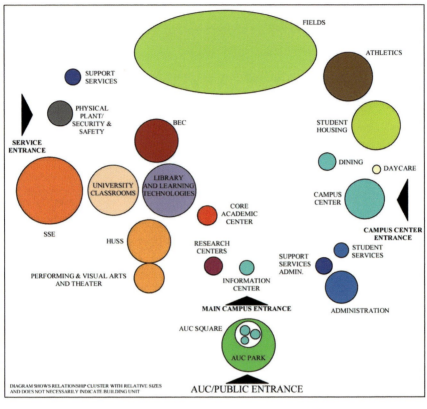

FIELDS

ATHLETICS

SUPPORT SERVICES

PHYSICAL PLANT/ SECURITY & SAFETY

BEC

STUDENT HOUSING

SERVICE ENTRANCE

UNIVERSITY CLASSROOMS

LIBRARY AND LEARNING TECHNOLOGIES

DINING

DAYCARE

CORE ACADEMIC CENTER

CAMPUS CENTER

SSE

HUSS

RESEARCH CENTERS

CAMPUS CENTER ENTRANCE

SUPPORT SERVICES ADMIN.

STUDENT SERVICES

PERFORMING & VISUAL ARTS AND THEATER

INFORMATION CENTER

ADMINISTRATION

MAIN CAMPUS ENTRANCE

AUC SQUARE

AUC PARK

DIAGRAM SHOWS RELATIONSHIP CLUSTER WITH RELATIVE SIZES AND DOES NOT NECESSARILY INDICATE BUILDING UNIT

AUC/PUBLIC ENTRANCE

DLM Campus Affinity Diagram
American University in Cairo (AUC), 1999

Sasaki Associates
Architectural Packages Diagram, AUC, 2005

AUC New Cairo Campus Photos, 2010

* * *

"The Campus Planning Process"

~ Arthur J. Lidsky, 2012

Planning is a decision making process—within a college or university it should be on-going and continuous. Often, it is seen as a one-time event. A campus plan is less effective if it is perceived as final —life is not that simple. All plans should be capable of changing as assumptions, circumstances, resources, and priorities change—as they assuredly will. The design of a building should anticipate change as well—especially a science building where changes in the disciplines and our knowledge of how students learn has had, and is likely to continue to have, a dramatic impact on facilities. Planning for a new building should not be considered an independent event, but should be done in the broader context of institutional planning.

Colleges and universities are a complex web of interdependent and interrelated programs, departments, individuals and communities of students, faculty, staff, and administrators all centered to some extent on the institutional mission. At the core is knowledge—learning it, creating it, sharing it, transferring it, transforming it, and storing it.

Mission describes the purpose of this wonderfully complex and creative organism called a college or university. Mission, the guiding purpose of an institution, changes rarely.

Vision, on the other hand, is about the future and, as such, is a critical and essential beginning to the planning process. It is a statement, consistent with the mission, about what the institution, the division, or the department wants its future to be—of what it will become.

One definition of vision comes from Bert Nanus, Professor Emeritus of Management at the University of Southern California. Nanus defines vision as a realistic, credible, attractive future for an organization.

Planning starts with a vision for the future. The vision reflects the mission and provides a sense of direction and a set of goals to be realized. The academic plan further defines the vision. It is here that the institution establishes its goals for the future, which include a point of view about such things as: new or changing degree programs, changes in faculty distribution, departments that will grow or change, programs to be nurtured, desired enrollment targets, student/faculty ratio, and faculty loading. All other institutional planning will flow from the goals, objectives, and priorities of the academic plan.

Planning, then, is a deliberate process to realize the vision. To be effective, comprehensive planning must weave academic, financial, and student life planning together with campus and facility planning. Of all these interwoven plans, it is the academic plan that is fundamental. All other plans within a college or university should be designed to accomplish the academic plan and thus the vision.

All college and university planning, whether for the entire campus or a single building, has the same constituent elements or steps. The more collegial the process (which it should be), the greater the participation of faculty, staff, students, and administrators, the more positive the outcome—and the longer the timeframe for developing the plan. Genuine participation, however, is essential for building consensus.

Coincident with the development of an academic plan, the institution should prepare an assessment of the current situation. A Strengths, Weaknesses, Opportunities, and Threats (SWOT) analysis is common during this step. So too is an audit and assessment of the existing buildings, campus, infrastructure, and environs and an analysis of the degree to which spaces, buildings, and environs support current programs and planned changes in learning, teaching, and research. At the same time, financial resources should be assessed in terms of such factors as operating costs, existing and planned capital costs, and deferred maintenance.

Benchmarking is a useful tool at this point. Comparisons to real and aspirational peer institutions is valuable data for decision making and for guiding planning discussions.

The academic plan becomes the embodiment of the institutional vision. The assessment of campus, facilities, infrastructure, and financial resources describes the current situation of the college or university. The next step in the planning process is to define the programmatic, financial, staffing, and facilities required to achieve the institutional vision. Essentially, this is a description of needs— prioritized needs.

Once the needs are described and prioritized, the institution can explore various alternatives for meeting the needs. These alternatives can be tested and costs and benefits developed. Those alternatives that more fully support the institutional mission, address priorities, and have a greater impact on achieving the vision will most likely be selected as first-phase projects.

The plan is then documented for fund-raising and for implementation.

It all starts with a vision and several fundamental questions: what do you want your students to know and be able to do? How do you want them to learn?

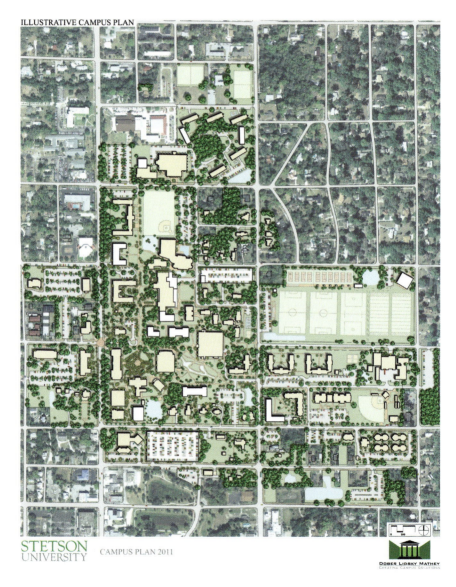

Stetson University Campus Plan
DeLand, FL

PART FOUR

STANDARDS, TOOLS, GUIDELINES

CHAPTER 4

"Design Guidelines - Integrating the Three Factors" ~ George G. Mathey, 2004

Campus design guidelines rooted in the precepts of the institution's mission are an excellent tool to integrate focus, finances, and facilities.

Too often, design guidelines are narrowly focused on ensuring that new construction will blend well with a campus's existing architecture and meet certain quality standards. While this is an important goal, a more powerful approach is to incorporate design guidelines as measures that encourage development consistent with your institution's strategic, academic, operational, and student life goals.

A Few Examples: If your strategy is to provide a "student centered education," including in your design guidelines directions to create student gathering areas—lounges, coffee bars, informal student work areas, email/internet kiosks (or wireless access points)—within buildings of all types would be a positive way to advance the goal.

If your academic plan emphasizes enhancing the institution's academic reputation through more effective faculty recruitment, your design guidelines could establish standards for faculty offices that improve this critical component of the institution's facility inventory.

If your institutional vision describes an "open, friendly campus accessible to all," the guidelines should include instructions to create facilities that meet the letter of the ADA, as well as to eliminate existing barriers in the project area. Another guideline should support the development of classrooms that are non-hierarchical and encourage student-to-faculty and student-to-student discussion.

If your operational goals outline the need for increased efficiency and lower costs for building systems and maintenance, the guidelines can help achieve that by suggesting building performance standards, and durable, easily maintained materials and finishes.

Process:

Creating mission-infused guidelines requires an expansive, collaborative approach that draws on a cross-section of campus leaders familiar with the institution's "non-physical" planning— faculty, administrators, students, and planners—so that the guidelines are informed by the institution's goals and can be drafted to inspire project designers to help advance those goals.

* * *

"Coherent Landscape Design"
~ George G. Mathey, 2004

Institutional image and an institution's campus are inextricably linked, whether one looks through Kevin Lynch's academic, analytical lens, or through the market-focused lens of the latest branding study.

What are the primary components of institutional image? The most vigorously pursued element is probably "reputation," typically rooted in the quality and distinctiveness of program offerings and the contribution made to intellectual and societal advancement.

The most diligently cultivated physical attribute is unquestionably an institution's collection of buildings. These buildings can simultaneously support programmatic achievements and endow them with a memorable physical expression.

One of the least emphasized physical elements is the campus landscape. The landscape provides the setting for buildings and the connections between them and to the community beyond the campus boundaries. Too often, the landscape lacks effective advocates and, therefore, funding. This makes creation and maintenance of the landscape an ad hoc, disjointed process. Landscaping then becomes building-related in its creation and maintenance is meager at best. Hence, a major asset and contributor to campus image is under-employed.

A thoughtful planning and design approach integrates architecture with landscape can help give greater presence to a campus with an unremarkable or highly varied character. Appreciating and coordinating landscape elements campus-wide—trees, shrubs, flowers, grass, benches, memorials, sculptures, plazas, paths, drives, and parking areas—can make a significant improvement in campus livability and image. Providing adequate funding and staff for continuous maintenance, renewal, and enhancement can knit the campus together with a rich, vibrant, useable, and handsome landscape setting.

* * *

"An Intentional Front Door" ~ Arthur J. Lidsky, 2005

How do you know which door to a building is the front door?

In many cases, the front door is an architectural gesture while other doors are used for day-to-day activities. Subtle and direct clues, cues, and cultural symbols combine to help identify the main entrance. These include landscape and pathways, an architectural element of glass and height, material, color, signage, and sometimes a platform and stairs. In ancient times in Egypt and Asia, large statues of gods and goddesses flanked the door and provided safety.

At the campus scale, a related question can be asked: does your campus have a front door—an easily recognized main entrance? Should it have? Some campuses have a definite main entrance— Furman University, for example has one of the most attractive.

Other campuses have several entrances, some more defined than others—St. Lawrence for example. A number of urban campuses have no discernable entrances as their buildings are often interspersed with other property owners and buildings making it difficult to define the campus boundaries. For M.I.T., the front door to the campus really is the front door to a building—77 Mass. Ave., under the Great Dome.

First impressions are important as students shop around for a college or university that they believe best meets their criteria, expectations, and biases. What impressions does a visitor receive when they arrive on your campus?

Although not all campuses have, or should have, a front door, visitors to the campus should know when they have arrived through physical and visual clues that help orient the visitor and guide them to their destination with parking nearby. A number of institutions have found it beneficial to have the Admissions office near the entrance, easily identifiable and accessible.

Furman University Entrance
Greenville, SC

* * *

"Tools for Planning II - Floor Plans, Inventories"
~ George G. Mathey, 2005

Every institution benefits from current, accurate, fundamental planning tools. After all, you can't manage what you can't measure.

Whenever space allocation, space utilization, or staff and department moves are on the planning agenda, up-to-date, scalable floor plans of key buildings (at least) are an essential tool (documentation of all buildings is ideal). These provide not only visual data regarding space available and the arrangement of space but also serve as the basis for a room-by-room facility inventory.

Facility inventories typically track:

- Building
- Room Number
- Room Use
- Department
- Room Area in net square feet
- Number of Seats (or assigned users, depending on room type)
- Occupant

Many other room characteristics can be tracked, but the above are essential. Many institutions have highly developed inventories, especially if they are required to report on space allocation to state or federal authorities.

Increasingly, these institutions are merging floor plan and inventory data in sophisticated Facility Management systems. Many other (most?) institutions have little or, at best, no current detailed space data, crippling their ability to know what they have, how it is allocated, and how space can be more effectively deployed.

Developing and maintaining this data is labor intensive, especially the first time it's done, and requires consistency of method and level of effort over time to be most useful.

Build budget for this effort into a major planning study that can cover it or focus an effort prior to a campus plan. With knowledgeable direction, you can use student help to make the project more feasible.

Source: Postsecondary Education Facilities Inventory and Classification Manual, NCES 92-165.

* * *

"Creating Car Free Zones" ~ George G. Mathey, 2006

A planning principle now accepted almost universally has been in force at our office for over four decades: keep the car in its place.

The car has a place, and its place is critically important. A community college cannot thrive without providing adequate, convenient, safe and plentiful parking. On residential campuses, purists would argue that most students have no real need for a car.

Often, however, institutions are reluctant to deny their students this "right," "privilege" or convenience if it might cause the prospective student to re-consider attending the school.

Urban campuses have an even greater need and incentive to control the impact of the car.

Let's grant the necessity of the car, but keep it in its place, focusing on management—making parking and circulation efficient, convenient and safe. The operational rationale is evident, but the real purpose is to ensure that the core campus can be a special environment, free of the distractions, noise, fumes, clutter and hazards of moving and parked vehicles.

A campus must be designed for the comfort, stimulation, delight, and safety of people. In our increasingly virtualized world, educational institutions have an obligation to create environments that encourage and celebrate people and their face-to-face interactions.

Focus effort on:

- Excellent Signage

- Demand Management—ride share, park and transit, scheduling
- Rationalizing Parking—adequate parking, perimeter lots, parking decks, short-term parking close-to-core.
- Policy Enforcement—consistent permitting, lot controls, ticketing, penalties.

* * *

"What's in a Word" ~ Arthur J. Lidsky, 2006

Optimize is a wonderful word. On a college campus you can optimize almost anything: resources, facilities, capital investments, views, information technology, opportunities etc, etc, & C.

So what should we optimize today? Classrooms! Classrooms have many measures to optimize: the number of scheduled hours per week, percent of seats filled, size, room configuration, location, acoustics, lighting, technology, furniture, and air circulation—to name a few.

Usually the issue comes down to whether there are a sufficient number of rooms. Those with fiduciary responsibilities often have the suspicion (or hope) that there are too many rooms. In contrast, faculty know that there are too few rooms and therefore classrooms should be added.

One widely accepted norm is that a typical classroom should be scheduled 30 hours per week assuming a 40 hour workweek.

Often, although there are 40 hours a week in which to schedule, many institutions cluster their classroom usage between the hours of 10:00 AM and 2:00 PM in response to faculty and student preferences. However, distributing courses more evenly across the day to avoid the usual clustering of courses will not change the average hours per week—it will only make scheduling easier.

If to optimize utilization means to increase the number of hours per week that the typical classroom is used then no amount of adjusting the schedule will suffice: the same number of classrooms and the same number of courses will always yield the same number of hours per week. The only way to increase the hours per week is to either have more courses (increasing faculty load and requiring a smaller section size) or reduce the number of classrooms.

* * *

"How-To"
Assembling the Basic Planning Tools III
~ George G. Mathey, 2006

For the planning team truly interested in how a place works and in how its physical plant can be adjusted to work better, base maps, floor plans, and facility inventories (details in Perspectives issues 3 and 10), the following information is essential:

- Institutional organization chart—It's tough to know the players and how they relate without a dramatis personae.
- Summaries of space allocation by school and department. These help illustrate how much space each unit has to work with, where the space is located, and what the range of space types is.
- Institutional staffing table—Information about the number of staff in each department for understanding the relative size

and scale of units.

- Teaching space utilization reports—Reports from the registrar's scheduling office indicating the intensity of classroom and teaching lab use for understanding and making recommendations for the teaching space inventory.

- Faculty and staff office locations—For understanding the pattern of the distribution of staff across campus.

These tools help planners begin to understand the internal dimensions of a school, college or university and answer questions like:

- How many classrooms do we have? How efficiently are they used?

- What are the range and average sizes of our faculty and staff offices? Where are the problem areas?

- Do our social science (athletics, student records, performing arts, admissions, humanities, student activities, physical sciences, residential life, etc.) departments have sufficient space? Who's really hurting?

- How can we address the key needs to achieve our strategic goals in an integrated plan?

Using these tools as a basis for analysis and recommendation steers planning away from the anecdotal towards the objective, enhancing a plan's transparency and acceptance.

* * *

"Standards, Standards, Standards, Everybody's Got Standards" ~ Arthur J. Lidsky, 2007

"The nice thing about standards is that there are so many of them to choose from." -Andres S. Tannenbaum

One of the benefits of facility standards and guidelines is that they provide a consistent measure applied in a variety of different circumstances. The use of the word "standard," however, carries the implication of having been vetted and accepted as right or appropriate. But who makes that judgment? How and when should standards change?

Most facility standards today are based directly or exactly on standards developed in the late 50s and early 60s. The early thinking of the Western Interstate Commission on Higher Education (WICHE) is evident. Some facility standards have not changed in over 50 years, even though dramatic change in technology, teaching, pedagogy, research, and our understanding about how people learn should have effected at least some of them.

An interesting example is the faculty office. In many states, the standard for a faculty office is still 120 net square feet. When that standard was set, desktop computers didn't exist—in fact, computers wouldn't show up on the desktop until 20 or 25 years later (Apple 1976 and IBM 1981).

This enduring standard shows the difficult evolution and slow response for facility standards in ever changing circumstances. It also shows a misunderstanding of the purpose and use of a faculty office. The faculty office is a personal work space as well as a teaching space, meeting place, and research area. It is a place to learn and discover. It is used to meet with students, staff, and other faculty. It is used for administrative functions. It is a dining room, a place to nap, and a space for contemplation.

In our office database of over 20,000 citations from colleges and universities, both public and private, the average office size is 145 net square feet. We have analyzed a number of faculty office sizes and configurations and recommend that a typical faculty office be in the range of 140 to 160 net square feet for most departments and institutions.

The typical college and university campus dedicates more space to offices than to classrooms. Institutions need to recognize this office space as a critical learning environment on campus—and treat it as such.

More importantly, though, it is time for State Higher Education offices and colleges and universities to take a fresh look at facility "standards" that are being used to define space. These institutions would not use old, out-of-date building codes to construct new buildings—why use out-of-date standards to plan them?

* * *

"Why Hiring a Star Architect Isn't Always a Stellar Idea" ~ Arthur J. Lidsky, 2005

One-time signature architects, or celebrity architects, are now called star architects, and they have a lot of fans in academe. Ever since people began to build shelter there have been prominent architects. The first we can actually name, however, is the Egyptian Imhotep, who built, for King Djoser, the Step Pyramid at Saqqara, the precursor of the iconic pyramids at Giza.

Today's architecture stars are glamorized like their counterparts in the personality cults of Hollywood and sports. And as in those other fields, their reputations rise and fall with their latest deals and projects.

There are more than 100,000 registered architects in America, but only a score of them are considered stars. What makes them so? Sometimes the news media anoint them. Sometimes they're awarded a prestigious commission. Sometimes they have the support of powerful architecture deans. Often they're just lucky.

Selecting a star architect doesn't guarantee the best design or the most innovative solution. It usually means the design will be unconventional, however. Does unconventional mean creative? Does it imply "the best"? It does to some.

In 2001 the National Arts Journalism Program of Columbia University surveyed 40 newspaper architecture critics in America. The critics' highest-ranked living architects were Frank Gehry, Renzo Piano, Santiago Calatrava, Maya Lin, Norman Foster, Steven Holl,

Tadao Ando, Richard Rogers, Rafael Moneo, and James Stewart Polshek. "Among the five least favorably rated architects," according to the report, "is a group of theory-oriented deconstructionists: Zaha Hadid, Bernard Tschumi, Greg Lyn, and Peter Eisenman." Nonetheless, all are considered stars.

Star architects have their place. The field needs those who will challenge us and will make us see buildings and spaces in new ways. But not all institutional buildings should serve that purpose, and not all colleges and universities can afford that luxury. Nor do they all have the skill, strength, and expertise to work with architects who have sizable personalities and powers of persuasion.

Working with a strong architect requires an equally strong client. Most colleges and universities are simply not up to the task. Many senior executives are inexperienced with construction, and few are trained to critically assess design. Moreover, it is easier for the college or university technical staff to go along with a design when both the architect and the design are strongly endorsed by the president or a board member. When—as often occurs—a project's budget increases beyond a stated and accepted limit, when facility plans increase and mutate without the administration's understanding of the implications for users, site, program, and operating and maintenance costs, senior administrative leadership has failed. Unique materials, unconventional angles, custom-design joinery and cladding are not only expensive to build but also require special care to maintain.

Star architects are very creative in describing their buildings. Steven Holl said that his design concept for the Massachusetts Institute of Technology's Simmons Hall came from a sponge, and that the building reflected the sponge's porosity. In reality, Simmons Hall is as porous as the Great Wall of China and, on the exterior, just as intimidating.

Sometimes star architects dazzle prospective clients by discussing projects as though they were brilliant abstract art. Even when we don't have a clue what the architects are talking about, we're impressed by their grand visions or swayed by their designspeak.

Try parsing this:

"In Santiago my idea was to superpose a Cartesian grid onto the existing, organic, medieval 'grid' and warp or deform them with a topological grid that projects upward. This produces lines of force that were never a part of projective geometry. They mutate in the third dimension. This has a powerful impact on the ground surface. It is a way of dealing with the ground not as a single datum, not as a foundation, not as something stable. It disrupts its iconic value, turning it into an index."

In the same interview, Peter Eisenman also said: "I do not do function." That's a problem if you want a functional building.

Colleges and universities should never give up control of their buildings. The institution should see to it that each building is true to its purpose, budget, schedule, and design. It is your building, not the architect's. It should meet your needs today and, more important and to the extent possible, your changing needs well into the future.

In the past college buildings were constructed for particular purposes, and usually for a particular group of faculty members. Today academic buildings should be designed not only to anticipate expansion but to allow for changes in space requirements, academic program, new forms of pedagogy, and evolving research and technology. Classrooms should be able to become offices, offices laboratories, and laboratories classrooms. The more singular the space, the more difficult it will be to renovate and modify.

Look, for example, at the Weatherhead School of Management's Peter B. Lewis Building at Case Western Reserve University. Frank Gehry was chosen with the hope that his design would physically put the school on the map—it was a conscious institutional marketing strategy. The original budget was around $25-million— the cost, however, grew to more than $60-million. There were no real constraints on the facility program or budget—particularly since a donor promised to pay 60 percent of the cost of the project but didn't place a cap on the cost. He heroically stayed with his promise, but the leap in cost clearly reflects a lack of institutional leadership. Yes, Gehry should have been more sensitive to the prescribed financial limits of his client and the original budget target, but what incentive did he have?

In their June 2002 *Civil Engineering* magazine article, "Structure as Art," Vincent J. DeSimone and Derrick D. Roorda describe the complex design of the Lewis building. A major design element within this brick building, which is crowned with cascading ribbons of stainless steel, are two classroom towers:

"At the bottom of each tower are three 3-foot (0.91-meter) square concrete legs, some leaning inward and some outward. The legs rise from the basement level, which is 20 feet (6 meters) below the surface. A large, irregular opening in the ground floor allows the legs to rise to the base of an irregularly shaped concrete slab about 50 feet (125 meters) in diameter and 15 feet (4.5 meters) above the ground floor. This slab forms the base of the bottommost classroom. Four 30-inch (762-millimeter) square concrete columns rise within each tower, leaning in different directions from the edges of the thick slab to support the upper classroom levels and the roofs above."

An elegant structure and creative sculpture—but as curriculum, programs, and technology change over time, how flexible and adaptable will this building be?

Two recent buildings at MIT also highlight some of the liabilities of working with star architects.

One of the interesting characteristics of the MIT campus is that no one building (other than I.M. Pei's high-rise Green Building) really dominates. Yet there is great architecture on the campus— some designed by other renowned architects: Baker House, quiet and understated, by Alvar Aalto; Eero Saarinen's chapel and auditorium; and, of course, William Welles Bosworth's iconic Great Dome entrance on Massachusetts Avenue.

But now two buildings assertively call attention to themselves and step away from the understated context: the newly completed Stata Center by Frank Gehry, and the antithesis of understatement —Simmons Hall, a 350-student residence.

In the 1960s MIT constructed its first and only high rise, the 21-story Green Building. Afterward the consensus was to avoid high-rise academic buildings since they constrain interaction by isolating faculty members. The taller the building, the smaller the floor plan, and therefore the fewer faculty members who can be located on each level. For many years, most new academic buildings on the campus were kept to no more than five stories. The Stata Center's two towers go beyond the five-story target, and also separate the faculty members into two buildings.

The Stata Center, a building of about 720,000 square feet, consists

The architect Steven Holl has said his design concept for MIT's Simmons Hall came from a sponge

MIT Stata Center Entrance
Cambridge, MA

of two nine-story buildings linked on the ground floor with a variety of public spaces and areas for informal gatherings and discussions. Below ground is parking for 700 cars. The center also integrates an existing swimming pool into the ground-floor public space. Plans for the center originally called for 150,000 square feet at a budget of $160-million. During design, the cost increased to more than $280-million.

The center provides space for the Computer Science and Artificial Intelligence Laboratory, the Laboratory for Information and Decision Systems, and the Department of Linguistics and Philosophy. Conceptually, the center, organized around a "student street" with vertical "neighborhoods," is supposed to foster interaction and multidisciplinary teaching and research.

Gehry creates sculptural architecture—or architectural sculpture. His building and designs use materials, structure, shapes, and spaces in ways that challenge our preconceptions. His use of computer modeling and titanium as a building material has allowed him to create radically untraditional works. Gehry's buildings are unmistakable.

Not all buildings, however, should be occupied, large-scale, pieces of sculpture. Within the next decade MIT will realize that its choices will hinder the users' ability to rearrange and modify their environment. Imagine the debate about ruining some carefully designed area when someone requests the construction of walls and ceiling to enclose a new research initiative, or needs to convert a public space into labs or expand with the insertion of an interstitial floor in one of the great, soaring spaces.

Simmons, like Stata, started with a smaller estimate of space needs. During the design process, because no real constraints were placed on the architect, the original facility program (the document guiding the architect and engineers on a project's fundamental requirements) changed in concept and grew, as did the cost of basic construction, fixtures, furnishings, and fees. The concept of porosity, stemming from the image of a sponge, led, among other things, to more than 5,000 two-foot-square windows that are almost guaranteed to become a physical-plant problem in a few years. And porosity? A fine word but meaningless in the reality of execution. The last public project-cost estimate that I saw was $92.5-million that's about $264,000 a bed, or the cost of a three-bedroom house in many parts of the country.

Most architects are, or should be, embarrassed if the cost of construction for their designs exceeds the budget targets and financial resources of their clients. And yet the costs of many star architects' projects have been significantly greater than originally planned. Why is that? I would think that solving an architectural problem within budget requires more, not less, creativity.

Choosing an architect because an institution wants something different, or wants to create excitement and "buzz," is shortsighted. How long will the buzz last? Five years? Ten years? Campus buildings have long lives—50 to 100 years. For a building to grow in size during the design stage is a certain indicator of poor institutional control. The size, cost, components, uses, and users should all be defined well before the design process even begins.

To me, a real star architect displays the genius of creativity while being sensitive to the client's needs, respecting the program, creating a building that can respond to inevitable change, and staying within schedule and budget.

A real star client respects, but is not in awe of, its architect, and knows when to say no.

Source:

The Chronicle of Higher Education

Section: Campus Architecture, Issue dated March 25, 2005

Volume 51, Issue 29, Page B18

PART FIVE

FACILITIES PLANNING

CHAPTER 5

"Uniting Institutional Needs and Vision with Architectural Design and Construction"

~ Arthur J. Lidsky, 2004

INTRODUCTION

A facilities program is an essential first step between a college or university's vision of new or renovated space and the realization of that vision through architectural design and construction. The program not only is a description of new or renovated space, but also is a valuable institutional management instrument for controlling cost and size and for ensuring that user intentions are met during the design and construction phase of the project. If the program is neglected or superficially prepared, *ad hoc* and often detrimental changes to the size, cost, configuration, and constituent elements of a project can occur during the excitement of subsequent architectural design phases. The facilities programming process can become a useful institutional forum for various constituencies to voice opinions and needs. As a result, through a participatory process, consensus can be achieved within the limits defined, ensuring a successful project. The programming procedure:

- Defines institutional and user requirements
- Defines the construction and project cost constraints
- Provides the necessary information for an institution to decide whether the project will entail new construction, renovation, or a combination of both
- Provides guidelines for site selection
- Reduces the probability of change orders and therefore reduces the probability of construction and project cost increases
- Facilitates the institutional process for gaining approval to proceed with the project
- Can be used for fund raising for specific donors
- Can be used to gain consensus
- Can be used to shape discussions about staffing, enrollments, curriculum, and pedagogy

ESSENTIAL ELEMENTS OF A FACILITIES PROGRAM

A facilities program consists of user descriptions of vision and intent, justification, and rationale for the project; site location information and diagram; space relationship diagrams; and a detailed description of each space in terms of purpose, size, architectural characteristics, building system requirements, location and proximity requirements, and furniture and equipment.

Figure 56.1 lists the categories used to describe each space in a facilities program. Readers are referred to Figure 56.5 for an example of a typical detailed room description.

Figure 56.1
Facilities Program Categories for Each Space

1. General Description	**2. Architectural Characteristics**
Space identity code	Windows
Department	Doors
Name of space	Floor loading
Probable occupancy	Floor, wall, and ceiling finishes
Hours of use per day	Ceiling heights
Net square feet	Acoustical requirements
Purpose	
3. Building System Characteristics	
Temperature	Lighting requirements
Humidity	Plumbing requirements
Room controls	Workstation requirements
Exhaust requirements/hoods	Communication requirements
Fire protection/suppression	Air pressure
Electrical requirements	Safety
4. Access and Spatial Relationships	**5. Special Furnishingstand Equipment**
Location and adjacencies	Furnishings
Access	Equipment
Security	Other requirements
	Special considerations

PROCESS

To be successful, the facilities programming process must be participatory, involving those who will use the facility as well as those who will operate, manage, and maintain the space. The process consists of eleven steps:

1. Selection of project and review committees
2. Articulation of working assumptions
3. Review of program, curriculum, and pedagogy
4. Analysis of existing physical resources
5. Description of needs preliminary list of spaces required
6. Comparisons to normative standards and peer institutions
7. Alternative combinations of new and renovated space
8. Best alternative
9. Summary program type, size, purpose, department, occupancy, height, proximity and location requirements for each space and project cost estimates
10. Institutional approval to proceed
11. Detailed program department vision and project concepts statements and a description of each space based on architectural characteristics (windows, doors, floor finish, ceiling finish acoustics), mechanical characteristics (temperature, humidity, electrical, lighting, plumbing, communications fire protection/suppression, security, elevator), and furniture and equipment requirements

Step 1: Selection of Project and Review Committees

The simplest approach to managing the facilities programming process is to establish one committee made up of six to nine institutional representatives. This committee will serve as a review group and conduit for formal and informal comments and reactions from colleagues as the work is made public and will approve the work, in principle, at the end of each phase of the programming process.

The composition of the committee depends on the type of project: academic, residential, academic support, administrative, student life, or some combination of activities. The committee should consist of faculty, administrators, and students formed to be representative while at the same time providing checks and balances. For example, if the building is to be academic and the majority of the committee are faculty members, care should be taken to broaden institutional representation by including faculty from departments that are not directly associated with the project.

On some campuses it is beneficial to have two committees. The one as previously described to focus on the specific needs of the users associated with the project and the second, a smaller committee comprising administrators and faculty, to be charged with taking the broader institutional view and based on an understanding of the campus wide implications of the project.

Project Manager Key to the success of the facilities programming process is the individual selected to be responsible for the day to day requisite tasks involved in shepherding the project through the programming and the design process.

The project shepherd is responsible for such tasks as scheduling meetings and ensuring that information, issues, and decisions are shared with users and institutional representatives. The project shepherd should become the institutional memory for the duration of the project.

At some point during planning and implementation, the project shepherd will need to have release time from other responsibilities to carry out the communication role that is inherent in this position. The timing for this will depend on the scale of the endeavor and the degree to which certain tasks can be delegated, but added responsibilities usually reach a peak during the design phase, which follows programming.

Facilities Programmer Facilities programs can be developed by faculty, administrators, in house professional staff with this expertise, architect, planner, or programming consultant. To a certain extent, the choice depends on the scale and complexity of a project and the skills, experience, and availability of in house personnel. Larger institutions typically have someone in facilities management or planning who can initiate the facilities programming process.

Whereas the project shepherd is responsible for communication and coordination, the facilities programmer is responsible for developing the program by working with the committee and user groups. The larger or the more complex a project, the more likely it is that a consultant should be engaged to assist in the programming process. A laboratory or theater facility, for instance, will require technical assistance not usually available in house. In some cases the project benefits from the objectivity and independent outside views that consultants can interject.

Step 2: Articulation of Working Assumptions

The second step in the programming process is agreement on the basic assumptions that will set consistent boundaries and guide the programming discussions.

Schedule Accelerating the process by shortening the schedule can lead to a superficially prepared program. A facilities program can be completed within three to six months depending on the campus's complexity and the need for collegiality and interaction of participants. Whatever the time limits, it is imperative that the programming process be participatory and participation takes time.

Time Frame Set the horizon for planning far enough into the future to broaden the users' thinking about facilities improvements beyond just the fixing of current needs. After all, assuming funding is available, given the typical time needed to prepare a program, select an architect, design a facility, construct new or renovate existing space, and finally move and occupy the facility is usually three to four years. If the horizon for planning is short, the resulting facilities improvements may be short lived.

A useful target for planning and programming purposes is 15 or even 20 years.

People A fundamental set of working assumptions that will inform and guide the programming process is agreement on the current and projected number of students, faculty, and staff associated with each of the departments affected by the project.

These projections must fit into the context of the institution's academic plan. It is easy, but can be unfortunate, to move into the "wishful thinking" stage mode at this point. A facilities program must be based on enrollment and staffing projections that are consistent with the institution's vision for the future.

It will be interesting to note the current number of faculty and staff associated with this project who might retire within the time frame for planning. Should the new or renovated facility be planned for the current or future faculty and staff?

In finalizing the numbers of students to be planned for, managers should be aware that a new facility often has a positive impact on the number of majors associated with the departments within the building. Once the new facility is operational, more students are likely to be attracted to those disciplines.

Dollars Construction and project cost estimates should be developed as part of the facilities programming process and compared to the anticipated financial resources that will be available. This is critical in that it adds reality to the programming discussions while informing the review and selection of alternatives.

The institution should decide on the amount of capital it can provide to support this particular project. The programming process will either confirm this amount as being on target, adapt the program to the resources, or provide adequate justification for modifying the stated amount.

Step 3: Review of Program, Curriculum, and Pedagogy

The beginning point for any discussions concerning new or renovated facilities on campus academic, academic support, or residential/ student life must be based on the institution's mission statement and academic plan, as well as on the current and planned curriculum and pedagogy. The objective is to identify the spatial implications of these factors. (*Academic* plan in this context is used as a synonym for the broad institutional plans that are developed for all programs on campus.) The questions listed below might be used to begin such discussions.

Mission Does the college or university have clear and articulated descriptions of its mission? Are the mission statements of the user groups consistent with the overall institutional mission?

Curriculum Does the institution have plans for developing new programs or for changing existing programs that may have spatial implications for the new facility? Will new majors or minors be introduced into current programs? Will existing programs be eliminated? Does the institution anticipate changes in graduation requirements or core curriculum? How should interdisciplinary teaching and research be accommodated? To what extent will undergraduate students be involved in research?

Teaching Methodology What are the institutional expectations for and policy on faculty and student research? Will the faculty course load policies, vis avis teaching and research, be modified? How will technology, computers, and multimedia be integrated into the curriculum and pedagogy?

Step 4: Analysis of Existing Facilities Physical Resources

To make informed decisions about facilities improvement or expansion, an understanding of the existing resources is necessary.

Facilities The parameters for planning improvements were identified in Steps 2 and 3. At this next step the college or university should thoroughly analyze and understand the amount, type, utilization, and condition of existing space by department or user group. It is difficult to make any judgments or decisions about the future use of space without this elemental data.

The amount of existing space should be compared to normative standards for room size and utilization. It is also useful to compare the amount of space available to departments or user groups with the amount available at peer institutions. Typical peer comparisons are usually in the form of total department space per faculty or student.

The existing condition of space should be analyzed both in terms of physical condition and conformance to codes, particularly life safety and Americans with Disabilities Act (ADA) regulations.

Besides providing information for long term deferred maintenance budgets, this analysis may also determine the future use of a building. In some instances the cost of renovation outweighs the value of the building and may even indicate that the building be replaced.

Another review entails an assessment of how well the existing facilities support the current and intended user activities. For instance, a number of science faculty are embracing a hands on, experiential style of teaching, with less emphasis on teaching in a lecture setting and more emphasis on flexible laboratory environments. Does the size, use, or configuration of existing space support faculty teaching and research?

Site Site opportunities and limitations are vital to any project that requires new space, whether a new building or an addition to an existing building. Understanding these issues, which include such elements as parking, service, vehicular and pedestrian circulation, landscape, and topography, is basic.

Step 5: Description of Needs

At this point in the process, the departments or user groups should develop a preliminary list of spaces required to support the department's or group's mission and plan. A simple summary list might look like the example in Figure 56.2.

Step 6: Comparison to Normative Standards and Peer Institutions

It is important to review the space requests to ensure that the list is inclusive, all spaces are needed, and the amount of space can be justified. The desire to ask for more space than is necessary can be balanced by a careful comparison to normative standards and peer institutions.

Figure 56.2
Example of a Summary of Space

Space ID	Space Type	Space Name	NSF	Number of Spaces	Total NSF
English					
ENG 1	310	Office, faculty	130	19	2,470
ENG 2	310	Office, department chair	180	1	180
ENG 3	311	Office, secretary	130	2	260
ENG 4	311	Waiting area	90	1	90
ENG 5	312	Office, student assistants (4)	200	1	200
ENG 6	350	Meeting room/conference (15)	375	1	375
ENG 7	355	Kitchenette, shared	90	1	90
ENG 8	315	Work room, copier	130	1	130
ENG 9	315	Storage	270	1	270
				28	4,065
History					
HIS 1	310	Office, faculty	130	9	1,170
HIS 2	310	Office, department chair	180	1	180
HIS 3	315	Storage	65	1	65
HIS 4	400	Microfilm reader, shared	130	1	130
HIS 5	311	Office, secretary	130	1	130
				13	1,675

Based on the preliminary list of spaces developed in Step 5 and fine tuned in this step, estimates of construction, project, and operating costs can be prepared to inform the review process. If project and operating costs are beyond institutional resources, than the preliminary list should be modified to bring estimated costs into line. The normative standards and peer comparisons can provide helpful guidelines in accomplishing reductions, if that is necessary.

Step 7: Alternatives

The college or university should, without getting into architectural design, explore alternatives for grouping the departments and user groups based on an understanding of the affinity and proximity requirements of each. These alternatives should incorporate an analysis of existing space in order to make full use of these resources, and can include combinations of new space, renovated space, and reallocated space.

It is at this stage that the site study is important in testing locations for new buildings or for additions to existing buildings. Often the lack of available land or unique site conditions determine the choice of alternative.

Figure 56.3 depicts an analysis that shows several constraints: steeply sloping terrain, special landscapes, and specimen trees.

Figure 56.3
Carleton College - Campus Planning Studies 1996

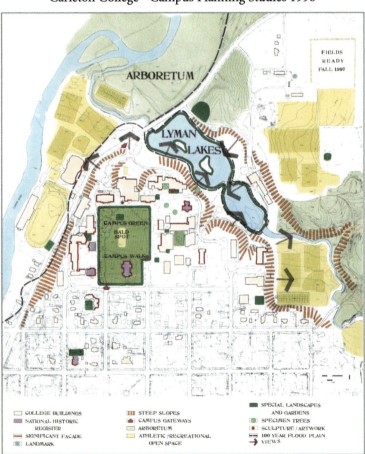

Figure 56.4 shows another type of site constraint: two buildings are to be connected for programmatic reasons with a building designed to fit within the given boundaries. In this case the allocation of existing and new space is critical to a solution where all three buildings must work together.

Figure 56.4
Washington and Lee University - Site Location Diagram

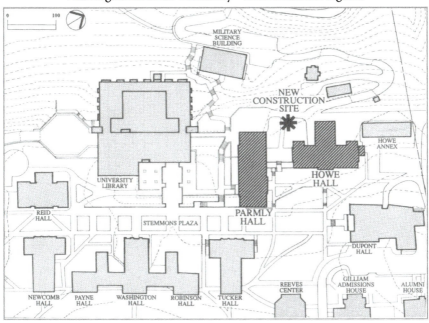

Step 8: Identification of the Best Alternative

One alternative should be identified and described in the program. Success in choosing the best one depends on carefully developing a set of criteria for judging. Criteria are specific to each situation but can include such factors as cost, total size of project, groupings of departments, the use or reuse of existing space, location, and effects on other institutional departments and units. This phase may involve several revisions as various elements are combined to produce the best alternative.

Step 9: Summary Program

The summary program states working assumptions, justifies need, defines the concept, lists the spaces to be included in the project, and estimates cost.

This information should be documented and compiled for campus review and approval. The program's audience should be the upper administration and, depending on the institution, the Board of Trustees.

Step 10: Institutional Approval to Proceed

If the programming process has proceeded as outlined above, two committees with a broad representation have participated. Moreover, the process of defining space needs, developing working assumptions, and reviewing alternatives will have involved a broad spectrum of faculty, staff, and students. The final concept will reflect input from many constituents and therefore should receive campus wide support.

Once the administration or Board of Trustees approves the program in terms of size, cost, location, and concept, then the summary program can be expanded into the detailed facilities program. Often the detailed information is collected concurrent with summary information. However, the detailed program should not be completed until after the summary program is approved.

Step 11: Detailed Program

Using the summary list of spaces as an index, descriptions for each space are then developed. Figure 56.5 shows an example of the expected level of detail. This information will include general space descriptions, architectural characteristics, building system characteristics, access and spatial relationships, and special furnishings and equipment.

Figure 56.5
Example of a Room Description

Rensselaer Polytechnic Institute	*Space Number*	*9*
Center for Polymer Synthesis	*Hegis Category*	*210*

General Space Description

Department:	Center for Polymer Synthesis
Name of space:	Lab, pilot/process
Net assignable square feet:	2,100
Number of spaces:	1
Total net assignable square feet:	2,100
Probable occupancy:	
Typical hours of use per day:	10

Purpose: Pilot scale facility for large scale chemical synthesis. Space includes a 300 NSF High Bay Reaction Room and a 400 NSF Control Room.

Architectural Characteristics

Windows: Required, operable sash, shades or blinds; observation window into Reaction Room.

Doors: Double 3' - 6"x7" without central mullion, master key, view panel; Double doors and access to exterior of building.

Floor loading: Laboratory loading

Ceiling height: 20' high in Reaction Room

Floor finish: Concrete with sealer

Wall finish: Ceramic tile

Ceiling finish: Sound absorbing, exposed to allow easy access to utilities

Acoustics: Not to exceed PNC 35 40

Figure 56.5
Example of a Room Description (continued)

HVAC, Electrical, Plumbing

Temperature:	630 to 760 F
Humidity:	No special requirement.
Room/zone controls:	Room control
Exhaust to outside:	Required, 18' walk in fume hood; elephant trunk exhaust manifold to service a variety of equipment.
Air pressure:	Negative
Electrical:	440V, 220V 3 phase, 110V grounded duplex outlets along walls, along counters at counter height, outlets accessible in floor; all outlets, switches, and fixtures should be explosion proof.
Lighting:	Fluorescent, non glare; high intensity lamps.
Plumbing:	Hot and cold water, sink, floor drain, cooling water for equipment; steam or hot oil.
Required communications:	Telephone, LAN, connections for voice, image, and data.
Safety:	Standard code, eyewash, emergency shower, sprinkler system, heat and smoke detection. Lab will contain hazardous chemicals in the form of acids/bases, flammable liquids, and oxidizers.

Access and Proximity

Proximity:	Adjacent to Processing Lab
Access:	Enter from adjacent corridor and Process Lab

Special Furniture, Equipment, and Other Requirements

Furnishings:	10 gal. kettle, extruder, molding press, mixers, etc.
Equipment:	Reaction Room should have decaliter distillation equipment; steam at 1,000 k Pascals (consider hot oil); refrigerant coolant; polymerization unit. The space should be high bay with 20' height. All electric outlets, fixtures, switches, and wiring should be explosion proof.
Other:	Reaction Room will house solvent recovery equipment; anticipate 1.6 gallons

Another useful component is a graphic version of required space adjacencies.

This type of diagram helps to further explain the relationship of one space to another (Figure 56.6).

Figure 56.6
Space Relationship Diagram

SPACE
RELATIONSHIP
DIAGRAM

ST. JOSEPH
COLLEGE

HUMANITIES
& ARTS

Access to
Music
Department

052
Music
Listening/
Resource
Storage

400

047
Language
Lab Office &
Storage

250

046
Interactive
Language
Lab

800

180

045
Language
Faculty
Offices (4)

007
AV Lecture Hall

048
Language
Resource
Room

375

180

044
International
Studies
Office

032
Slide/
Video
Viewing

180

180

031
Art History
Faculty
Offices (2)

033
Slide/
Video
Collection

180

059
Religious
Studies
Faculty
Offices (4)

180

064
Seminar/
Meeting
Room

400

058
Philosophy
Faculty
Offices (2)

180

063
Faculty
Lounge

200

180

043
English
Faculty
Offices (4)

Key

— Circulation (through and/or vertical)
→ Entrance
— Adjacent
- - - Near
(000) Space and Net Area

N.B. Faculty Offices to be clustered by
discipline. Location on diagram is
not intended to denote special order.

061
H & A
Secretary

150

049
Honors
Program
Office

180

062
Workroom

120

065
Foyer/
Exhibit
Hall

180

060
Adjunct
Faculty
Offices (3)

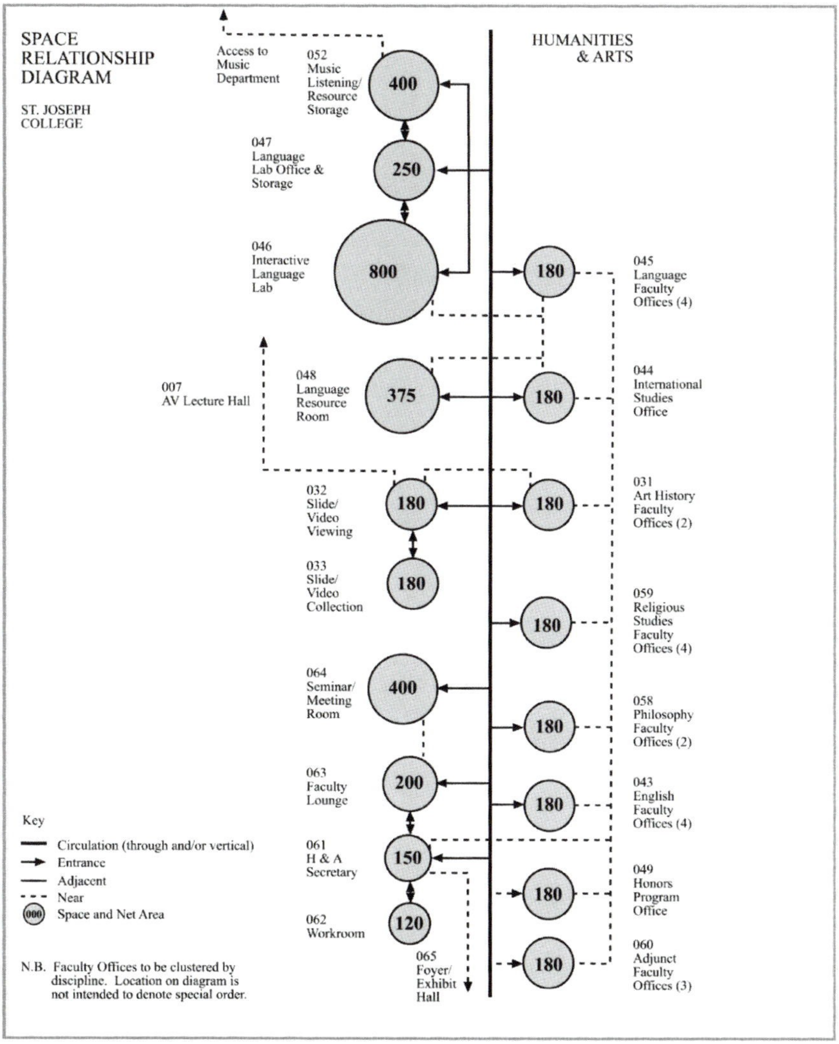

The audience for the detailed facilities program is the architect and engineering team. For the college or university, this document clarifies expectations, becomes a framework for assessing architectural designs as the design and construction drawing phases proceed, sets the limits of the project scope, and ensures a product that will meet the needs of the users.

Source: *"Facilities Programming: Uniting Institutional Needs"*
Published in the 1997 third edition of APPA's 4-volume set, Facilities Management: A Manual for Plant Administration
Reprinted with permission of APPA, Leadership in Educational Facilities

* * *

"The Ever Changing Campus: Pedagogy, Technology, and Facilities"

~ Arthur J. Lidsky, 2004

Pedagogy (the art and science of teaching), technology, and facilities are intricately intertwined. They each affect the other—and each has changed dramatically in recent years. Over the past 30 years, research on how people learn has made great strides. Moving beyond theory, this research is beginning to have a significant impact on teaching, the approach to student learning, and the facility resources required.

Even more than pedagogical change, technology has, is, and will continue to be a rapidly evolving tool used for teaching and learning. Colleges and universities need to have a strategy for providing facilities that will respond to and support this continuously changing resource, as well as the changes that are occurring in learning.

This article will explore the characteristics and types of facilities that will be required to support these new pedagogical and technological initiatives.

Pedagogy

Research has shown that there are more effective ways to facilitate learning than the traditional teaching. Lecturing to passive students who are busy taking notes is less effective than actively engaging students in their own education. Engaged, active, hands-on, problem-based, and project-oriented are all current terms used to describe an approach that recognizes that students learn by doing. The goal is to encourage critical thinking and the understanding of concepts—not the memorization of facts, dates, and figures.

Two examples of current active learning initiatives at the undergraduate level are Workshop Physics at Dickinson College and project-based learning at the College of Wooster. There is growing support for undergraduate research at many institutions, and dramatic changes are taking place in introductory courses, particularly in the sciences.

Colleges and universities are supporting these programmatic initiatives in many ways. One is a more appropriate and sophisticated approach to faculty development. Formerly cast in remedial undertones, faculty development centers are becoming laboratories for faculty experimentation and learning, staffed by professional educators and information technology specialists. The Anderson Center of Undergraduate Education at Rensselaer Polytechnic Institute is an example of this evolution.

Academic fields are also changing. The scope of classic and familiar disciplines is expanding, and new disciplines are being created. Thirty years ago, none of the following departments existed: bioinformatics, biomedical engineering, cinema and comparative literature, earth and space science, ecology and evolutionary biology, genome sciences, information infrastructure, management science and engineering, and molecular technology.

Today, these and other such departments are becoming commonplace. With them comes the need for new types of research space, located to advance interaction among faculty, students, and staff with relevant interests.

The number and complexity of centers and institutes, the

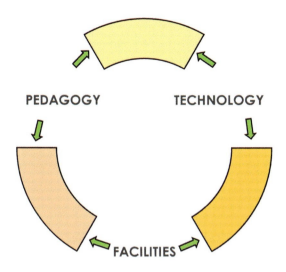

interdisciplinary organizations common to universities, has increased significantly since the early 1970s—from about 6,000 to about 13,000. Most have facility needs ranging from simple office space to major buildings. In the recent past, changes in facilities were being driven more by technological and programmatic change than by changes in enrollment. Over the next 15 years, however, enrollments are expected to increase by 15 percent as the Baby Boomers' baby boom moves through the primary and secondary school system.

Technology

The most startling changes are in technology. It was only 27 years ago (1977) that the Apple and Tandy computers were first introduced, and 23 years (1981) since the IBM PC reached the market. Ten years ago Netscape was introduced and the Internet became an incredible resource linking institutions, corporations, individuals, and information in ways that were inconceivable just shortly before. Only nine years ago, Microsoft entered the so-called browser war with Internet Explorer.

In this relatively short period, the way we work, teach, communicate, interact, and do research has changed. So, too, has the way we design and construct individual buildings and whole campuses.

The average age of college or university students today is between 22 to 24. For these students there never was a time when computers didn't exist. Having grown-up with Game Boys, cell phones, PDAs, and the Internet, they expect their educational experience will be technologically advanced and accessible.

Computers, laptops, and handhelds will become faster, cheaper, more complex, and more pervasive. They will continue to change and evolve and be integrated into the learning environment. Colleges and universities should expect to continuously upgrade these "edge" tools. Because a greater proportion of students will bring their own devices, institutions will have to decide what they will provide to supplement student machines and to support the academic program.

The rapid advances in wireless technology—increasing speed and security—will mean students can use their computers anywhere on the campus. Students will be able to create instant, networked, learning environments wherever and whenever they wish. A group of students might meet in the campus center, dorm, or outdoor quad and create a small networked community focused on an assignment, project, or laboratory experiment. It might be serendipitous, but there certainly is a coming together of the opportunities created by a wireless network and the pedagogic initiative of collaboration and community learning environments.

There continue to be exciting developments in display technology. Digital projectors are no longer the province of the so-called "smart classroom," as they are becoming a mandatory and expected resource in all classrooms. The SMART Board is also no longer cutting-edge, combining whiteboard, computer, and projector with a touch-sensitive display that can save text and graphics to a computer file for printing, e-mailing, or Web display.

The CAVE (Cave Automatic Virtual Environment) is a new technology that will find its way onto many campuses in the next few years. It is typically an eight- to ten-foot cubicle where high-resolution graphics are displayed on three walls and the floor creating a three-dimensional virtual environment. Hardware and software can keep track of a person moving in this virtual environment and change the image accordingly. Do you want to walk through the arteries of a virtual heart or be in the center of a virtual space station? How about walking into a room that you are designing?

One of the most interesting new technologies involves the use of haptic devices. A haptic device allows a user to see and reach into a virtual three-dimensional environment and seemingly touch, feel, and manipulate an object created by a computer. A student wearing haptic gloves can pick up and hold a virtual three-dimensional molecule. The student can pull the molecule apart and reassemble it in various ways, and in pulling it apart can feel the "tug" of atomic attraction much they way one feels the force between two magnets being pulled apart.

Online communication, either through the campus network or the Internet, has led to online academic programs, electronic office hours, interactive assignments, Web-based projects, and formal and informal communities of learners. It is not uncommon for faculty from several institutions to jointly teach a course over the Internet to students. Nor is it uncommon for one professor to teach a course over the Internet to students at several colleges or universities.

Sharing expensive and sophisticated scientific instrumentation over the Internet is becoming more prevalent as their costs increase and the need for specialized technicians grow.

Facilities

The design and construction of academic buildings has shifted dramatically over the past 30 years. This shift is in response to changes in pedagogy and technology and the need to ensure that academic buildings can accommodate current and future initiatives. These facilities must allow change to occur at minimum cost and with little disruption. In the past, they were designed for specific faculty and programs. It has become clear that the more a design caters to individuals, the more inflexible and the quickly dated it will become. At Middlebury College, at least one third of the laboratory space in their new science building was designed as generic, division-owned space.

Classroom

Fifteen or 20 years ago, the typical classroom looked similar to the way classrooms have looked for the previous 50 years. Many new and renovated classrooms today are the result of pedagogical shifts and technological advances. They are different in size, configuration, furnishings, and technological equipment.

To differentiate between traditional classrooms and the newer, technology- rich classrooms, many colleges and universities use the term "smart classroom." That distinction will disappear as most classrooms are brought up to current standards.

Reflecting the shift toward engaged, interactive student learning, some faculty are moving away from the lecture style of teaching to a seminar or discussion format. This format requires a flexible classroom where students face each other around a table, in a circle, or a U-shape design, requiring more space.

Laboratory

Nowhere have the changes in facility design been more dramatic than in science, technology, engineering, and math departments (STEM). From a teaching standpoint, these fields require a lab-rich, hands-on, experiential, project-oriented collaboration of students and faculty learning and doing research together. Research used to be at the graduate level only, but today is a component of programs at undergraduate institutions and secondary schools.

The new style of teaching, learning, and collaboration requires a physical environment with flexible, movable benches designed for groups of two, four, or six students working together. In addition, some labs are being designed for both a discussion area with movable seating as well as a lab bench environment with small group benches, enabling faculty and students to move back and forth between discussion and experimentation. Labs of this nature require more space per student than traditional labs.

STEM spaces are also affected by the increasing number of computers and by the specialized, complex, and sophisticated equipment required for contemporary teaching, learning, and research. Much of the equipment now occupying floor and bench top space didn't even exist 30 years ago.

Office

Under the misguided notion of efficiency, a number of states have guidelines for the size of faculty offices based on a misunderstanding of the purpose of these spaces. Unlike offices used by industry, faculty offices are multipurpose teaching, research, and administrative spaces. There is growing pressure to increase the size of faculty offices to respond to changes in pedagogy and technology. Whereas 100- to 120-square feet per office used to be a typical guideline, faculty offices are now more likely to be in the 140- to 160-square foot range.

Library

Librarians as professionals and libraries as places are going through the greatest transition—and are still in the process of becoming. Becoming what, however, is still unclear as soul searching and experimentation continue to define and redefine the library. A library is no longer viewed as a passive depository for books and solitary scholars, but as an active, service-oriented, technology-based resource for collaboration and learning.

Computers in libraries have increased radically and the creation of "information commons" such as at the University of Arizona, are becoming important centers for learning and interaction. The information commons integrates information specialists, technology specialists, multimedia specialists, library resources, and technology resources, in an individual and group learning environment.

Some libraries are trying to make the library more comfortable and inviting. Clemson has introduced a small café, for instance. Other libraries, such as at Worcester Polytechnic, are moving some books off-site to make room for technology and small group study and collaboration spaces.

In the world of education, as in life, change is constant. A significant difference with the past is the speed with which change is occurring. Today, campus buildings must be designed to anticipate change through thoughtful decisions about building systems, building materials, structural bay size, room configuration, sight lines, room locations, and careful consideration about furniture and equipment.

Colleges and universities must continuously strive to reinvent themselves to become or continue as preeminent places for vibrant, interactive, transformative programs for teaching and learning. Flexible and adaptable facilities will play a pivotal role in creating environments to attain that goal.

Source: *"The Ever Changing Campus"* Published in the March/April 2004, *Volume 20 Number 2, Facilities Manager Magazine.*
Reprinted with permission of APPA, Leadership in Educational Facilities

* * *

"Facility Renewal" ~ George G. Mathey, 2004

Campus plans rightfully focus on the big picture—accommodating enrollment growth, supporting new programmatic initiatives, enhancing an institution's image, resolving significant problems of access and vehicular management, or determining the highest and best use of newly acquired land.

Yet essential background routines that support campus operations, promote preservation of institutional heritage, and convey institutional values such as stewardship are important also. Include them in your campus plan as actions and describe them collectively as facility renewal—building re-use, program-driven renovation, and remediation of deferred maintenance—to ensure vitality at your institution.

*Spring Hill College
Mobile, AL*

*Before:
Batting Cage in the
core campus*

*After:
One of an array of
AV classrooms
with collegial
gathering space at
classroom entries
(below)*

Building Re-Use

Building re-use typically follows the complete relocation of a function to new space, leaving a building vacant. Often, this sequence provides planners with an exciting opportunity to completely re-define a facility while accommodating a function that has clear links to campus plan themes and needs.

Actions such as converting an early 20th century gym to a 21st century student center, transforming a library to an on-campus guest house, re-conceiving an underutilized campus chapel as one of a range of new uses, or recovering an obsolete science building as a new humanities center are all examples of campus plan renovation initiatives. All of these are opportunities for the institution to revitalize core campus buildings to serve new functions in a manner sympathetic to campus plan and style.

Program-Driven Renovation

Many older campus buildings remain fundamentally appropriate for their current use, but require a significant renovation to better support evolving programs: adjust room sizes and adjacencies, provide new room types, and update and upgrade systems that support the building and its new arrangement. These actions aim at extending the useful life of facilities central to the institution's mission—an important campus planning goal.

By incorporating these projects into the campus plan agenda, the institution links the programmatic to the operational while preserving campus heritage providing an obvious fund-raising appeal.

Remediation of Deferred Maintenance

Campus plans should also reflect ongoing efforts to draw down the backlog of maintenance projects. One reason to include these projects in a campus plan is that the initiatives described above may alter the deferred maintenance project list with large-scale renovations addressing many maintenance issues in a facility. Another reason is to place these facility needs in the broad context of the campus plan.

Historically, dollars for facility maintenance are among the hardest to allocate at levels sufficient to catch up and stay current as maintenance is a never-ending and mundane process, rather than a transformative one-time event. Referring to these projects in the campus plan keeps the deferred maintenance issue before the board, the legislature, and on-campus decision-makers. More fundamentally, the stewardship involved in such projects is an important value that durable institutions should promote as it not only preserves institutional legacy, but makes budgeting more predictable, ensuring that your institution is not robbing Peter's essential maintenance program to support Paul's exciting and strategic new construction program.

Keep all of these needs on the table to ensure your institution's entire facility inventory best reflects its intellectual and organizational vitality.

*　*　*

"Integrating Space Needs Assessment

~ George G. Mathey, 2006

In discussions with people we meet on campuses, a commonly-repeated question is "What is the most important element of a campus plan?" My best answer is make sure the physical planning is supported and informed by a strategy-driven, comprehensive needs assessment and projection. This includes an evaluation of the space available on campus and its effectiveness in meeting program, strategic and operational needs.

This level of analysis is extremely valuable to the process. Some key reasons:

- The analysis provides substantiated findings to support key recommendations
- The demands of the analysis demonstrate a rigor that appeals to academic participants and plan reviewers (i.e., the faculty, senior administration, board, donors and oversight agencies)
- The findings often spark debate and constructive thinking that leads to insight and breakthrough/Aha! results
- Collecting the data and actually using it to develop information that all can understand and appreciate engages participants and observers from across the college on multiple levels

In these ways, a robust space needs assessment not only reinforces integrated planning, it also acts to integrate, through the process and its results, a wide spectrum of the college community in an activity very constructive to strategic improvement.

By a robust space needs assessment, I mean doing much more than simply crunching space numbers by space type and comparing them to normative or system standards or benchmarks. I mean doing much more than the very helpful, but insufficient, utilization study for teaching/learning spaces that indicates simply the hours per week classrooms and labs/studios are used and the percentage of seats filled. A truly integrative assessment should include:

- an in-depth analysis of space assigned to all academic

Findings - Space Needs Summary

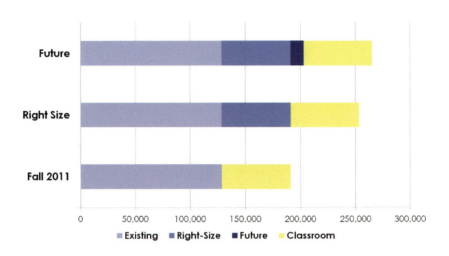

Findings - Space Needs Summary by Type

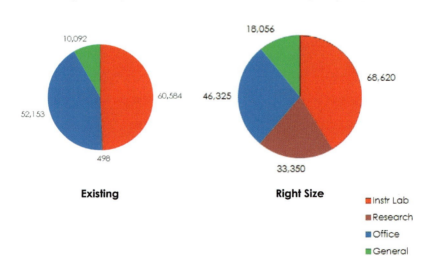

departments and administrative/support units

- a qualitative analysis of the spaces—how well they support current use and what is the best future use to advance strategic goals

- a thorough understanding of program needs that can only be built up through conversations with department representatives and campus leadership

- recommendations for future space allocations and required/ desirable renovations

- a calculation of the per-square-foot costs of maintenance and operation, renovation and new construction, adjusted by space type as needed—introducing costs into the conversation is a powerful attention-focusing technique.

These elements and the meaning and detail they deliver to a campus plan is the best way to ensure that the campus plan is something greater, more meaningful and long-lived than a glorified site plan.

Institutions are being asked to bring more rigor and accountability to the pursuit of their mission and the management of their campuses. Integrating this type of serious space needs assessment with your physical campus planning is one of the most effective ways to promote transparency and demonstrate the inter-connectedness of your campus, academic, financial, human resources and strategic planning.

Findings - Space Planning Principles

Departmental Space

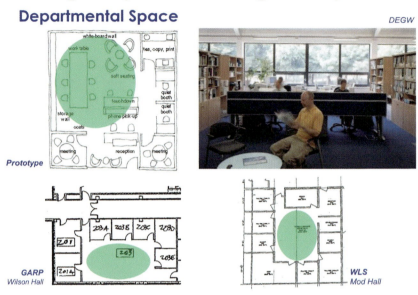

Prototype

GARP
Wilson Hall

DEGW

WLS
Mod Hall

PART SIX

STUDENT LIFE

CHAPTER 6

"Student Impressions" ~ Arthur J. Lidsky, 2004

Choosing a college or university is often a mystical correspondence of the rational and the irrational—the emotional and the cool. A prospective student's decision making process is, at times, neither obvious to the intellect nor apparent to parents. It's like falling in love.

So how does an institution influence a prospective student's impressions of the campus?

Consider these factors:

- The impression of the campus environment, buildings and land
- Admissions offices that resemble residential living rooms
- Student tour routes that admissions officers carefully craft
- The unfortunate institutional fad to use star architects to create an architectural statement, i.e., building as sculpture

But students perceive the campus in a more complex and sophisticated way.

- The quality and strength of the academic program and the institution's reputation.
- The perceived accessibility of the faculty and the sense that the administration listens.
- The racial make-up of a campus and the extent of diversity.
- The perception of a college or university's social life, informed by friends, siblings, the media, and apocryphal tales.

Still, one of the strongest—ignored—influences affecting student impressions of a campus is the subtle, personal connection created by the student tour guide. How the guide feels about the campus and expresses that feeling will have a significant influence on the perspective student's perception of the institution.

Do you want to have a significant impact on student perceptions? Do a better job of selecting and training your student tour guides.

* * *

"A Rationale for Campus Life Improvements"
~ George G. Mathey, 2005

Historically, colleges and universities have been perceived almost universally as places. Indeed, until very recently, what goes on at these institutions has been inseparable from the physical environment that supports, symbolizes, and sustains the activities. This unitary concept is, of course, changing as the national and global education environment evolves. On-line universities and distance-ed programs at place-based institutions, and other approaches that de-couple time and place have established themselves as significant forces in higher education. In a comprehensive survey conducted by the National Center for Education Statistics, 56 percent of all 2- and 4-year institutions offered distance-ed courses in the 2000-2001 academic year. An additional 12 percent were planning to offer such courses in the following 3-year period[1]. And according to the 2005 Chronicle of Higher Education Almanac, The University of Phoenix on-line campus has the fifth-largest enrollment of all US institutions with 48,085 enrolled.

Interestingly, it seems that the most successful of these institutions recognize that programs that are delivered only remotely do not provide optimal outcomes. As described by the leaders of two of the best-known cyber-providers at different SCUP plenary sessions over

---

1   Distance Education at Degree-Granting Postsecondary Institutions: 2000–2001, NCES 2003-17, E.D. Tabs.

New academic buildings increasingly provide social settings as opportunities for students to become engaged in a well-rounded curricular and campus life, shown here, the Science Education Technology Building at Cabrini College, Radnor, PA

Many established institutions are constructing facilities to foster student engagement and interaction, shown here, the Smith College Campus Center, Northampton, MA

the years, these institutions complement their on-line offerings with place-based activities that facilitate face-to-face interaction of students and faculty[2]. Listening to these sessions supports the notion that there is a real human need for personal, physical, eye-contact interchange to truly support learning.

Place-based institutions have always recognized this and have increasingly realized that the richer the campus life experience is, the more complete the interaction is, the more compelling the experience can be, and the more profound the possibilities for learning. Institutions that are heavily residential are the classic examples of the type. With a "captive" population, these institutions have the opportunity, indeed, the responsibility, to create a distinctive community and a range of experiences that the student perceives as wholly unique. The intensity of life in such a community can be, by turns, exhilarating and exhausting, but, most importantly, all consuming. People have a fondness for their college years largely in response to these dynamics, which are (some would say thankfully) not readily replicable in later life.

Place-based institutions must pay attention to the campus life experience they provide. Increasingly, this factor distinguishes them in higher education. On-line institutions can provide the content, delivering it with ever-improving effectiveness through always-advancing technology. They can provide equivalent content for fewer dollars than place-based institutions. What they cannot provide is the rich, all-consuming campus life experience that enhances and stimulates learning. Creating a dynamic, challenging curriculum

---

2   Diana Laurillard, Pro-Vice Chancellor (Learning Technologies and Teaching) at the Open University in the United Kingdom, SCUP 34 - Atlanta 1999, and Laura Palmer Noone of The University of Phoenix, SCUP 36 - Boston, 2001

conceived and taught by committed faculty in an environment that uniquely supports learning is the obligation and privilege of place-based institutions. The richer the experience, the more profoundly influenced students are and the more tightly bound they become, committing themselves to supporting the institution that afforded them such a thrilling, all-absorbing time in their life. If the mission-oriented rationale needs help, this financial reality helps provides it.

Clearly many, if not most, institutions understand this. After all, the range of campus life facilities and opportunities on most campuses is impressive and represents a major investment. For smaller institutions of modest means, however, there is still progress to be made. Academic and residential facilities will always be predominant in mission-driven institutions, but campus life facilities and programs are the essential third leg of the stool that solidly supports learning and living at our campuses.

* * *

"Keeping Up With The Joneses or Serving Student Needs" ~ George G. Mathey, 2005

In our practice, we have a close view of the front lines in the competition for students, faculty, and alumni support. The Higher Education (HE) sector's remarkable vitality and drive in improving institutions' appeal for support is impressive in its scope and accomplishment.

- undergraduate science labs that surpass cutting edge research facilities of the 80s
- student housing that rivals 4-star hotel accommodations

- small college athletics/fitness/wellness/recreation centers that the majority of national Olympic programs covet
- administrative and faculty office buildings that Fortune 100 executives would be proud to call their own

Student centers that are urban microcosms offering a staggering array of activities, services, and venues for entertainment. How does all this square with HE mission statements? Do high-end facilities truly improve student learning and development of personal strengths? Or are the "palaces" merely irrelevant, costly evidence of a demented "edifice complex."

Well, Mark Hopkins's only facility requirement was a log to sit on to engage the student sitting on the other end. Good for the Hopkins student, because that's all the finest teacher of his generation needed.

What terms do today's students and faculty stipulate? Most liberal arts faculty I've asked say the most important thing in job satisfaction and their career decisions is the quality of the student body. Likewise, committed students mention the reputation of the institution (the quality of the faculty), the "feel" of the place (the facilities and grounds).

Facilities and environment create a strong pull on students. Logically, then, the more attractive the facilities the stronger the pull; the stronger the pull the more selective the institution can be; the more selective an institution is, the stronger the pull on faculty; the stronger the pull on faculty, the better the faculty is likely to be; the better the faculty is, the stronger the institution's programs and reputation; and so on in continuous improvement cycle.

While the specific characteristics of the facilities may or may not provide measurable benefits for advancing student learning, that the facilities are perceived as being effective is taken as strong evidence of

MIT Stata Center Entrance
Cambridge, MA

Lecture Hall (below)

the institution's commitment to its mission and its students' success. These qualities will provide the necessary traction on students and faculty, strengthening the institution.

The facilities' impact on attracting and retaining the best requires a mission-driven investment. By assembling the strongest student and faculty groups possible, HE institutions are acting vigorously to enhance learning and the impact they have on students' lives.

* * *

"The Changing Focus of Student Housing"
~ Arthur J. Lidsky, 2010

More often than in the past, student housing is being used by colleges and universities as a continuation of the learning experiences and as a way to increase student attraction and retention.

Student housing can be divided into three broad categories: shelter, residential, and an integrated model of academic and residential life. Shelter, historically, is the predominant style of student housing on many campuses. Essentially it is a dorm in the stereotypical image double loaded corridor, mostly doubles, gang bathrooms, and little else. Many of these dorms were constructed during the 1960s and 70s. They were inexpensive, constructed quickly, and did what they were designed for: to provide shelter to a large number of students.

The second category of student housing is residential. Various amenities are provided—lounges, laundry, study rooms, etc.—a step up from basic shelter. It is the residential model that Student Affairs and Residential Life like to use in response to our changing culture

College of Wooster
Wooster, OH

Austin Peay State University
Clarksville, TN

and student (and parent) expectations.

The third category of student housing bridges the academic focus of an institution with residential life. Academic Affairs and Student Affairs coordinate, a variety of programs emerge, and the design of student housing changes to reflect these initiatives. In part, this is in response to the recognition that a diverse student body requires a diversity of housing options. In part, it reflects the institution's desire to eliminate or soften the students' sense of a separation between an official in-class experience and the students experience outside of structured academic activities.

The main trends that I will comment on are: First Year Experience, Privacy, Suites, Apartments, Learning Communities, Expansion of Amenities, Sustainability, and Privatization.

First Year Experience has been around for a long time and it varies by campus. On some campuses, it is simply a short-term activity as part of the orientation of first-year students. On others, it is a semester long or year-long series of seminar and events. On some campuses, the focus is similar—all first year students read the same books and hear the same guest speakers. On other campuses, the first year experience depends on the interest of the faculty who lead the session. Often the first year experience has a residential component where students in a particular seminar also live on the same floor or the same residence and can continue the interaction beyond the schedule class. Usually classroom or seminar spaces are provided in the residential environment.

Many student affairs/residential life offices support the notion that there is a process that all students must go through to become acclimated to the college culture—to living and working within the larger academic community. Having all first year students living in the same buildings facilitates the presentation of focused programs and events. It is also important that these students have roommates to ease the socialization process. Rooms therefore are usually doubles or triples. Many students however, have never shared a bedroom and would prefer a single room. The proportion of single rooms is on the increase as colleges respond to student preference.

Privacy Suites the trend toward the provision of suites has been slowly increasing, but now many campuses are being creative in how they define a suite and how it is designed into both new and renovated space. In its simplest form, a suite is two rooms, singles or doubles—sharing a bathroom. A step up from this concept is three rooms - with or without a bathroom—where the middle room is a social space and the two side rooms are bedrooms—again singles or doubles. This is the most common configuration for a renovated double loaded corridor dorm where every three adjacent rooms becomes a suite. In this scenario, in a renovated building, the number of beds is reduced by a third. Essentially, a suite is a number of bedrooms—singles, doubles, or a combination - and shared living space.

Apartments—the only space missing from a suite is the kitchen. Once the kitchen is included, the suite becomes an apartment. Apartments are used to provide a diversity of housing choices—typically for the older student. They can be located anywhere on campus, but usually apartments are sited on the edge to give the impression that they are off-campus, while still being on campus. Apartment style housing is sometimes provided as a way to bring seniors and grad students back to campus.

A variation of apartment living is truly off campus, either by design or the strategic acquisition of an existing apartment complex. There are some colleges and universities situated in cities and towns where large apartments complexes, privately owned, are providing a resource for the institution. In some cases, it is hard to distinguish between privately owned and campus housing. Some of these complexes have established a bus service shuttling students to campus and back.

Learning Communities—The expansion in the number and kind of learning communities is the strongest indication of the integration of student housing with academe. The annual survey of learning communities (National Survey of Living-Learning Programs 2007) had responses from 60 institutions with a combined total of over 600 learning communities. A learning community can be as simple as a theme house with no special space requirements or curriculum to a more complex center within the housing environment that includes classrooms, labs, small group study spaces, faculty offices, and related support. The strongest learning communities are integrated into the curriculum with courses that are required as part of Gen Ed and might be tied to a particular group of disciplines.

The importance of clear learning outcomes and assessment is an essential characteristic of an effective learning community.

Expansion of Amenities—It is interesting to see the amount of net square feet per bed increase over the years from the shelter model to the academic/residential model. In part, it is in the increase of amenities that are now considered standard. Some combination of the following spaces are becoming common: bicycle storage, communication closets, fitness/exercise, game room, kitchenette, laundry, music practice, public restrooms, recycling/receiving, residents' storage, trash holding, vending, and lounges of various forms.

Sustainability—I'm not sure what to say about sustainable practices in design, the choice of materials, construction practices, and every day operations of the campus. In ten years we won't even talk about sustainable issues—it will be commonplace—standard acceptable practice. There is an important pedagogical/student development issue here—the modeling of a sustainable lifestyle that shouldn't be forgotten.

Privatization—this could be a major report in itself. We are seeing more interest and more actual projects as colleges and universities try to find ways to provide more or better housing without adding significantly to their debt or operating budget. The issues center on ownership, construction and quality, and management. There are large corporations—developers—who are experienced in creating student housing for colleges and universities. Usually the developers design and construct the housing on land owned by the institution. The financial arrangements are varied but the most successful are those where an institutionally affiliated non-profit foundation is involved to keep the project off-budget.

The type, quality, and condition of student housing can make or break a perspective student's decision about whether to submit an application. In the future, we will see an increasing number of creative approaches to providing safe, comfortable, and diverse student housing.

PART SEVEN

TOWN/GOWN

CHAPTER 7

"Planning to Strengthen Town Gown Relations"

~ George G. Mathey, 2005

Neighbors' Impressions: A Spectrum

Noxious neighbors

Acquisitive, aloof, autonomous, and averse to paying taxes, providing student beds, and creating sufficient parking spaces. These are just some of the serious issues. Noisy, nocturnal students, game-day boorishness, and know-it-all professors compelled to offer opinions on community issues persist as some of the minor offenses.

Wonderful neighbors

Who else can provide such meaningful educational programs for adults and children, research to address an increasingly complex world's difficult problems, high-quality hospitals, intellectual and cultural activity, outreach programs for disadvantaged populations? On the lighter side, these organizations generate pride and connection through sports and association.

Where your institution's image falls on this spectrum of neighbors' views may depend primarily on the latest event that draws attention to the school. Regardless, the essential issue is trust, and the various planning processes—strategic, financial, and physical—can be conduits for building trust through direct communication.

Municipal Government

Campus planning staff should develop sound relationships with their counterparts in municipal government. Those responsible for physical planning should attend planning board/commission meetings on a regular basis (even when no issue directly affecting the institution is up for consideration). These kinds of actions are really the only way to develop understanding and a sense that there are common goals and approaches that can succeed. Establishing this relationship will also make bringing institutional interests before municipal authorities less confrontational.

Neighborhood Associations

Likewise, if abutting neighborhoods have advocacy associations, the institution's planners should attend their meetings to demonstrate interest and identify shared concerns. Typically, there are more issues that can be addressed to mutual benefit, than there are disagreements that divide. Some broad areas of common interest are:

- Neighborhood stability
- Safety
- Attractiveness
- Provision of municipal services as needed
- Economic vitality
- Strong school system
- Affordable housing

Working with communities and neighbors alike to advance these interests will build the trust necessary for productive communication.

Two Schools - Two Approaches

Institution A

- Large, well-established, research university
- Resource rich
- Secretive
- Un-communicative
- Programs that engage community not well known or understood by community
- Engenders suspicion
- Reflexively resisted

Institution B

- Small, young, focused program university
- Tuition-driven
- Communicative
- Emphasizes common goals
- Admits uncertainty
- Building trust
- Listened to
- Supported

While part of the picture sketched above is a case of topdog/ underdog, in the community meetings describing the developing campus plan with Institution B, a real sense of dialog exists with an appreciation of being mutually-dependent (or, at least, interested) equals. Rather than trying to ferret out the hidden agenda, the neighborhood groups can concentrate on working with the institution to improve things for all. Of course, having established and fostered these relationships is no guarantee that specific projects will sail through community group and municipal review. But all involved do think it improves the quality of exchange and holds potential for constructive progress.

* * *

"Transformative Initiatives – Positive Approaches to Working with your Community"
~ Arthur J. Lidsky, 2008

One of the first recorded conflicts between a college and a community was in 1209 at Oxford College. Another was the three-day battle on St. Scholastica Day in 1355, also at Oxford. It started in a pub—and rolled out into the street.

No wonder that the campus was designed to separate the townsfolk from the students.

Today, more than ever, being a positive member of your community is more than self interest. To do so is not a gift, nor is it charity, but an important aspect of long-range comprehensive planning. Creating an environment where the campus and community are at peace with one another has an important influence on student and faculty attraction and retention.

The Radcliffe Quadrangle
University College Oxford
Oxford, England

Areas of community concern are varied, but they usually can be categorized as follows:

- Distrust
- Drinking
- Fear
- Flight of Homeowners
- Increased Cost of Renting
- Land Acquisition

- Mistrust
- Noise
- Parent-owned Housing
- Parking
- Partying

- Payment-in-Lieu of Taxes
- Reduction of Property Values
- Reduction of Tax Base
- Student Behavior
- Student Housing

- Transient Nature of Students in Community Housing
- Traffic
- Trash
- Vandalism
- Zoning Charges

The quality and extent of an institution's community engagement depends upon the effectiveness of its presidential leadership. Early faculty and Board buy-in is essential to the success of any such undertaking as well.

Working with your community can be as simple as the College of St. Benedict's efforts to improve downtown St. Joseph or Macalester College's High Wind Fund. Started in 1956, the High Wind Fund now has an endowment of $13 million, and a mission "…to maintain and improve the beauty, serenity, and security of the area surrounding the campus." Projects include buying, renovating, and selling property in the immediate area of the College.

More complex efforts can be found at Trinity College's Learning Corridor, the University of Pennsylvania's West Philadelphia Initiative, and Clark University's University Park Partnership. In all three cases, the institutions, in partnership with a variety of city, state, and federal agencies have transformed their neighborhoods. And in each case, it was the president of the institution that led the effort.

The University of Pennsylvania's initiative was lead by President Judith Rodin. She created five strategies for the area: economic growth, business development, improved housing, a "clean and safe" environment, and quality of schools. The University helped to create the cutting-edge Penn Alexander School—a public pre-K through eighth grade school for 500 students. In addition, the University partnered with utility providers, unions; and block associations to light 1,200 neighborhood porches and build parks in University City, the University's neighborhood. Two programs were directly involved—UC Bright, which began as a collaboration between the University and PECO, Pennsylvania's largest utility; and UC Green, which supports greening in University City and other Philadelphia neighborhoods. UC Brite subsidized the installation of homeowner lighting and street lighting for over 150 blocks in the area, and UC Green provided trees, shrubs, and plantings.

The University initiative provided mortgage incentives to faculty and staff to buy and improve homes in the neighborhood and bought and renovated houses to return to the market. New businesses, shops and restaurants; a grocery store; and a movie theater were subsidized and a special-services district with extra security and garbage collection was created.

Saint Lawrence University's Canton Initiative has had equal impact, but on a different scale. The University has provided loans to retail operations within the city, has helped establish a coffee shop and restaurant, and has promoted the renovation of historic town buildings. The University has also assisted Habitat for Humanity and the Women's Health Center. In another interesting move that benefited both town and gown, the University exchanged the closing of a Canton street that bisected the campus for contributing to downtown parking improvements and funding for a city fire station, a Canton Child Care facility, and for construction of new housing units.

There are several public-support organizations that have focused on campus and community issues over the years. Campus Compact focuses on community service, civic engagement, and service learning. http://www.compact.org/ The work of Campus Compact includes faculty, staff, and student training; research on effective programs and practices; advocacy and policy work on issues; and grants, funding, and awards.

The Town and Gown Association of Ontario is another example http://www.tgao.ca.

Clemson University and the City of Clemson have proposed that a National Town Gown Association be created as a primary source of information for common issues between institutions and their communities.

∗   ∗   ∗

"Public-Private Partnerships for University Housing Development" ~ Erika Johnson, 2010

In the realm of campus development, public-private partnerships are becoming a more common occurrence, but are nothing new. The trend began nearly 20 years ago as cash-strapped colleges and universities looked to the private sector to assist with the construction of student housing. Private development had been used previously to construct bookstores, student centers, and offices, so upon a key IRS decision in the 90's, housing was the next natural extension of this arrangement. Private developers, with knowledge of real estate markets and the development process, saw that their skills could marry well with universities' tax-exempt status, land holdings, and constant stream of tenants.

Universities are finding that this is a beneficial arrangement for a number of reasons. For one, it provides the obvious advantage of deferring the delivery and budget risks to the developer as well lessening the impact of the debt to the university's books. This also makes the developer solely accountable for completing the project on time. When students sign contracts for the housing months in advance, they and their parents fully expect to move in at the designated date before the semester begins. If a project gets behind schedule and the facility is not ready for occupancy on day one of the contract, the developer is charged with finding suitable accommodations, usually in a nearby hotel, and arranging transportation to campus.

This partnership structure also leads to a more manageable bidding process that greatly reduces the amount of time and money needed to go from project inception to completion. As opposed to a standard process, whereby the university bids out separately for planning, design, and construction services in stages, with public-private development the university issues a single RFP for full-service developer-led teams. The developer is able to assemble a specialized team of architects, engineers, and contractors and leads the process while working intimately with university administration. The value of this type of integrated planning is that it allows for the entire team to discuss design and specification issues as they happen, rather than requiring the construction team to loop back with the design team over discrepancies, helping to keep the project on budget and on schedule. The development and construction process is also more streamlined because the developer is required to guarantee the design to the exact specifications agreed on by the University at a guaranteed maximum price.

Georgia , like a number of other states, does not provide public funding for housing development, which leads most public colleges and universities in the state to pursue public-private partnerships to increase their housing stock. In particular, Georgia Southern University in Statesboro, Ga. has built 2,900 new beds since 2003, each with varying design programs and rental rates, to attract undergraduate students to on-campus living throughout their college years. The most recent project to open is Centennial Place, completed in partnership with Ambling University Development Group, which includes 1,001 beds in apartments and suites as well as 10,000 SF of retail space. For this development, GSU's third public-private housing development, the University set up a separate single-purpose non-profit LLC to own the project. GSU manages and maintains the property as part of its current housing program, with the LLC board providing oversight of the building's finances and repair costs.

In the end, it's the institution's students, faculty, or staff, not the development team, who will be the users. As Vickie Hawkins, Director of Housing for Georgia Southern University, states, what is most important in the relationship is to choose a developer that is willing to treat the university as a customer and work collaboratively. "When disagreements arose on issues such as how much money was allocated to the project, interpretation of the contract, or interpretation of the University's architectural standards, the clear, open, and honest communication as well as the strong working relationship that the university and developer had established was the key to effectively resolving these issues. You cannot have an adversarial relationship and get what you want out of the project." The university's administration has to be very involved with decisions on the design and material selection throughout the project.

Hawkins, who has been with Georgia Southern University for 30 years, offers the following advice for institutions seeking to enter into a public-private partnership.

- Each state and university is different. Find out how your state addresses public-private development and what your college or university administration desires from the project before moving forward. Some trustee boards are more willing to take on risk than others to control the development process and outcome. Also, contact others who have been through the process to see what worked and what didn't to get information that will help you make the best decision.

- Ensure that the RFP is as comprehensive and specific as possible so that developer teams know what you are seeking and what to expect from the project. Ensure that the contract is strong with clear language to help avoid disputes because, in the end, the contract guides the process. For the University and the developer, the detailed architectural design specifications provided a high level of clarity so that Ambling knew what GSU wanted and GSU also could refer back to the standards when disagreements in design came up. The specifications went from the broad to the specific, including items such as the type of surveillance system to install and bathtub faucets. Ensure that you work with a developer team that values open communication, an honest working relationship, and collaboration to work out problems and keep everyone on the same page.

• Set expectations of one another at the beginning and review them every few months to see how well you are meeting them.

Public-private partnerships do not work for all campus housing projects, but they do allow universities to drastically increase the stock of on-campus housing and other revenue producing campus facilities without relying on public money or donations. While it is too early to understand the long-term implications of this type of development, to date it has allowed a more efficient and collaborative process that can create a winning formula for both the universities and development teams involved.

PART EIGHT

ACADEMIC
ISSUES

CHAPTER 8

"Creating Intentional Learning Environments"
~ Arthur J. Lidsky, 2006

At most colleges and universities, classrooms are only 5 percent to 10 percent of the total space on campus—that's a small amount of space dedicated to teaching and learning—particularly when many institutions think of classrooms their primary teaching venues. Certainly, some state agencies think so as evidenced by fairly restrictive utilization requirements to "improve efficiency." Laboratories, studios, offices, libraries, and student residences are among other learning spaces—formal and informal.

I'd like to talk a little about "intentional learning environments" beyond the classroom—but I want to move away from how the term is commonly used today. A Google or Yahoo search of the phrase "intentional learning environments" almost always comes back with another phrase: "computer supported" as a prefix. There are other intentional learning environments that I would like to highlight as they provide non-classroom and non-laboratory experiences.

A coffee kiosk at the College of Wooster is operated by students—a great learning experience for students and an easy way to distribute this type of food service to buildings that might be distant from dining and student union resources.

Students at a number of campuses are involved in all aspects of sustainability from simple recycling programs to campus life dorm sales, food scrap composting, pollution and prevention, energy use, and transportation.

Colleges and universities are moving towards having a complete wireless campus—Columbia University and the College of St. Benedict, for example—making learning and communication possible anywhere on campus—indoor and out.

On some campuses there are chalkboards or whiteboards in corridors or lounge areas, and even outdoors (at Carleton College), to support the spontaneous learning moment.

Many campuses have "living/learning" residences that combine housing with academic programs and academic support spaces.

The faculty office has become an extremely popular environment for learning, either on a one-to-one basis or in small groups. Libraries are finding there is a great demand for small-group studies where students work and learn together.

Middle Tennessee State has an outdoor astronomical plaza where the patterns on the ground and the upright sculptures are all designed to teach or to be used in experiments about the earth's rotation, planet and star locations, and moon and sun characteristics.

St. Lawrence University hires students to work side-by-side with the directors (project shepherds) of design and construction projects

University of Chicago, Chicago, IL
Graduate School of Business
Caseroom

University of Chicago, Chicago, IL
Graduate School of Business
Group Study

University of Puget Sound
Tacoma, WA

Old Dominion University
Norfolk, VA

for new and renovated buildings. The students are involved in the process from the early stages of facility programming, through design and construction.

The Swarthmore College campus is an arboretum with most trees on campus named—it is both an outdoor lab and museum.

The first year experience—usually a seminar—can have a residential component on some campuses where students in a particular seminar also live in the same residence allowing discussions and interaction to continue beyond the formal meeting.

The student union at Gettysburg College is run primarily by the students, and is an opportunity to learn about organization, funding, budgeting, politics, and consensus.

The general operations of a campus often have students involved, from grounds upkeep and maintenance, to technology and networking. Students work at the computer center help desk, they tutor, and they are involved in community service, student government and a myriad other activities in which learning occurs.

Yes, the classroom is important—its design, furnishings, technology, size, and configuration can support or hinder communication and learning. But learning takes place everywhere on a campus. Thought must be given to how students learn, and where, so that those environments can be just as intentional as the classroom.

* * *

"Interdisciplinary Conditioning"

~ George G. Mathey, 2009

In the past twenty years, one of the most frequently-stated academic and facility goals I have heard is the need to create or renovate buildings to encourage interdisciplinary work.

Partly a reflection of evolving funding mandates where government and foundation support is contingent on an collaborative approach to research or instruction, interdisciplinarity has taken on the near-mantric formulation that cutting edge work will, by definition, involve more than one of the "traditional" academic focus areas.

As a planner involved with campus design and facility development, I don't feel qualified to judge the validity of this assertion, but I can observe that there are few facility and campus plans created in the last two decades that have not held this notion as a key plan driver.

The facility responses have included innovations such as:

- providing more small and large group meeting spaces
- ensuring a mix of departments in buildings, wings, floors and "pods"
- creating "commons" spaces with amenities to encourage informal, spontaneous faculty and student interaction
- developing dramatic atriums where occupants and visitors can "see and be seen" coming and going on their daily rounds spurring chance encounters
- creating generic, flexible lab and other research spaces that

can accommodate, with reasonably straight-forward

adaptation, a wide range of discipline-specific requirements

While such building features can no doubt enhance collaboration, institutions should ensure it by:

1. providing leadership and incentives to make clear that work across disciplines will advance rather than deter a faculty member's career trajectory, and

2. reducing organizational barriers (or "lowering the walls" to borrow a phrase in common use at the University of North Carolina Chapel Hill),

3. hiring and nurturing faculty that have shown an aptitude for productive collaboration.

Alan Grossman, a senior faculty member at the Harvard Business School, suggested the importance of individual interest and capabilities in overcoming institutional barriers. If the work achievable through collaboration with others is worth doing, creative, committed, organized people will make it happen. As an illustration, he related an instance of collaborating with colleagues in the Graduate School of Education on a research study and the development of a book detailing the study. A road-block arose early on in the process when it became apparent that sharing files on School servers using University networks would be impossible—faculty from one school couldn't access servers maintained at the collaborating faculty members' Schools. Their solution was simple, if somewhat unorthodox—like many a church group, dog lovers club, or youth soccer league, they created a Yahoo user group and got on with their research and writing.

While thoughtfully-designed facilities can no doubt support and enhance collaboration, institutions should first ensure the

Middlebury College
Middlebury, VT

Harvard Business School
Harvard University
Boston, MA

Harvard Kennedy School
Harvard University
Cambridge, MA

(also below)

optimization of such facilities by creating an academic environment supportive of interdisciplinary work and the development of a faculty that knows how to play well with others.

* * *

"Policies and Interdisciplinary Goals"

~ Arthur J. Lidsky, 2009

If a goal of your college or university is to encourage interdisciplinary teaching and research, are your institutional policies hindering this objective?

Tenure and promotion requirements are a major impediment to interdisciplinary programs as they encourage silos, narrow interaction, and discourage initiatives between departments.

When your institution is interviewing candidates for a faculty position, do other departments participate in the selection? Do they have a vote? A number of institutions now require that any new hire help another department.

If several faculty desire to teach a course concurrently, does the way in which faculty credit is given support or hinder that activity? At some institutions, faculty will get full credit despite the shared initiative.

Faculty load also plays a part in that the higher the load, the more likely that teaching will be a priority. Finding the time to explore and create interdisciplinary courses and creating opportunities for interdisciplinary research will not be a priority.

How does the institution deal with cost recovery when several departments are working together on a research project? Is it assigned to the PI's department, shared, or allocated based on some other factor, such as the number of graduate students involved or a percentage of the research expenditure?

Geography plays an important constraint as well. On many campuses, large departments have their own buildings, almost guaranteeing isolation. In the future, there will be fewer stand-alone buildings and more interconnected spaces.

So while space provides the opportunity for interdisciplinary initiatives, without a careful review of the policies that might impede its implementation, the opportunity might be lost.

✳ ✳ ✳

"STEAM"

~~STEAM Power, Blow off STEAM, Get Up STEAM, Under One's Own STEAM, STEAMed Up, Run Out of STEAM, Full STEAM Ahead~~

Rats, all the good titles are taken

~ Arthur J. Lidsky, 2009

From *A Nation at Risk* in 1983, to the *Neal Report* in 1986, to the 2007 *Rising Above the Gathering Storm*, to President Obama's emphasis on STEM education—the need to improve how we educate students and how students learn has been talked about, criticized, supported, standards created, and standards modified.

There are various indicators which show that the U.S. educational system—elementary, secondary, and higher education—has fallen behind a number of countries. In a 2010 study published in the British paper, the Guardian,   470,000 15-year olds from 65 countries were tested for reading, math, and science knowledge and skills. The U.S. ranked 17th in reading, 31st in math, and 23rd in science[1].

During the past thirty years or so, a large and growing body of knowledge has developed about how we learn and the various ways to encourage and support student learning—not only in K–12 but in post-secondary education as well.   There is recognition that students must take responsibility for their own education. That students learn best when they are actively engaged.   There should be a balance between working individually and working in teams or small groups. There is a benefit to integrating knowledge across disciplines.   What we have learned and are continuing to learn is to have an impact on pedagogy, curriculum, and facilities.

Last year the National Research Council of the National Academies published a book titled A Framework for K–12 Science Education which recommends three dimensions for a framework:

- 1 – Scientific and engineering practices
- 2 – Crosscutting concepts that unify the study of science and engineering through their common applications across fields
- 3 – Core ideas in four disciplinary areas:
  - o   physical sciences
  - o   life sciences
  - o   earth and space sciences
  - o   engineering, technology, and application of science

---

1   Source: Organization for Economic Cooperation and Development

"Old Faithful Geyser" Yellow Stone National Park, WY
Photo by: Yvonne Santos

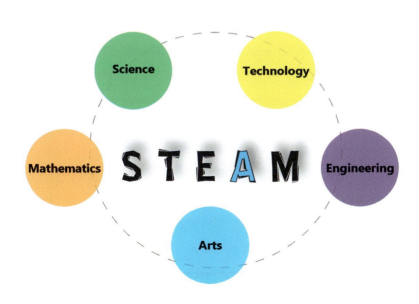

Now educators, teachers, faculty, researchers, and parents are exploring another initiative, widely dubbed STEAM. There is growing interest and increasing experimentation in merging the STEM disciplines with the arts. Someone very cleverly created the acronym STEAM to represent these initiatives. The literature has a variety of cute titles playing with the word Steam. So we have Steaming Ahead; Building Steam; Steam Heat; From Stem to STEAM; etc. But the notion of integrating the arts with the sciences is not new. In fact, we can go back several centuries to Archimedes or to Leonardo da Vinci—to the artist/scientist—to the Renaissance man.

There have been a number of movements integrating the arts with science or engineering. In the 1960's, 70's, and 80's there was collaboration between engineers and artists—Experiments in Art and Technology which grew to more than 20 chapters throughout the country. But these were professionals bridging the disciplines, whereas STEAM is a rethinking of the way in which we educate students in the sciences and the arts.

The objective of a STEAM curriculum is to foster the true innovation that takes place when combining the perspectives of a scientist and an artist[2]. The idea is not to convert a scientist to an artist or to force an artist to be a scientist. Rather it is to open the student's mind to new ways of seeing and experiencing the world. It is to train, encourage, and nurture creativity and innovation—whether it is defining an experiment, building a device, creating an app, solving a math problem, or sculpting an artifact.

Colleges, universities, and schools are exploring these disciplinary overlaps as a way to enhance student learning and to foster creativity.

---

2   I am using the artist to include studio arts, performing arts, writing, crafts, etc.

Important research on learning and a STEAM curriculum is developing at Brown, Duke, Harvard, RISD, RPI, San Diego, Stanford, UCLA, Vanderbilt, Wesleyan, and Wisconsin.

The STEAM Journal is being hosted by the Claremont Graduate University.

Experiences across the country have revealed that education is best met in hands-on, experiential, lab-rich environments with project-based curriculums which will produce teachable moments and a community of learners.

In his 2008 article *(Arts Foster Scientific Success: Avocations of Nobel, National Academy, Royal Society, and Sigma Xi Members)* in the Journal of Psychology of Science and Technology, Robert Root-Bernstein looked at all Nobel laureates between 1901 and 2005, the Royal Society members from 1932 to 2005, all National Academy of Science members from 1877 to 2005, and two avocation surveys of Sigma XI between 1936 and 1982. Equating Sigma Xi with the typical scientist, the study showed that members of both the Royal Society and the National Academy were significantly more likely to have an avocation in the arts and crafts. More revealing, well over 90% of the Nobel laureates were or are engaged in the arts as an avocation.

"After a certain high level of technical skill is achieved, science and art tend to coalesce in esthetics, plasticity, and form. The greatest scientists are always artists as well." —Albert Einstein

The American Association for the Advancement of Sciences (AAAS) had a panel discussion about "Artful Science" organized by John Jungck, who is the Director of Interdisciplinary Science Learning Laboratories at the University of Delaware. The University of Delaware has created a new Interdisciplinary Science and

Engineering Laboratory focusing on the environment and energy. Laboratory teams will include biologists, mathematicians, artists, and policy specialists.

So what are the facility implications of STEAM?

One interesting implication is the similarities in building characteristics—a properly designed science building and a properly designed arts building have similar needs and requirements—HVAC, for instance, as well as structural bay sizes, the storage of chemicals, treatment of dust, and a higher than normal floor to ceiling height. Another is the need for flexibility and the ability to modify the space. This is true for most academic buildings, but more so for science and the arts. A number of campuses have former science buildings that have been renovated for the arts—Carleton College, for instance.

Another implication is the need for common community spaces and the careful placement of these resources to encourage serendipitous meetings.

It is easier at the secondary school level for both arts and science departments to be located within the same building—the scale is different than at the college level—they have smaller departments and no research space. The Madeira School in McLean, VA is embracing STEAM and is planning a combined building for the sciences, math, studio arts, and theater. There will be one, shared office for the faculty, combined labs and seminar spaces, and the sharing of various student breakout rooms and collaboration areas.

The Whitehorse Hall for Arts and Sciences at Everett Community College is designed with science labs within an inner block of space while art studios are placed along the periphery.

The new Structural and Materials Engineering Building at the

University of California San Diego is a true STEAM building with the Department of Structural Engineering, Department of Nano-engineering, Visual Arts Studios, the Center for Interdisciplinary Science for Art, Architecture, and Archeology, and the Center for Medical Devices and Instrumentation. A number of small centers that blur the boundaries between engineering and art will also be within the building. In addition to this innovative building, the University is offering a Master of Education in Science, Technology, Engineering, Arts, and Mathematics.

On many fronts—primary, secondary, and post secondary—there are numerous examples of initiatives that are crossing boundaries and creating interdisciplinary programs and facilities to encourage the blending of science and the arts.

I really hate to say this, but it looks as if STEAM is gathering steam.

* * *

"The Maker Movement" ~ Arthur J. Lidsky, 2014

Primary, middle, and high schools are creating Maker Spaces, so too are colleges and universities.

What's going on? What are these spaces? Why is DARPA[3], with $10 million, funding the creation of these spaces in a target of 1,000 high schools? Why are libraries also anxious to provide these resources?

---

3   Defense Advanced Research Projects Agency

For a long time now, we have known that active learning is an effective approach to enhancing the educational process. Just look at how the SCALE-UP[4] Lab has been embraced by many campuses. Most of these labs are variations of M.I.T.'s TEAL Room—Technology Enhanced Active Learning.

Learning by doing has been a mantra in the sciences for just as long or longer. But it has only been in the past decade or so that the confluence of the physical, digital technology, and pedagogy has come together. Whether it is called make space, hackspace, inventive lab, design lab, or STEM to STEAM, it is variations of the same concept.

It is really interesting how the idea of making something has become such an important movement that spans education from primary, to secondary, and higher education. It's as if higher education has finally realized what teachers in primary schools have known for years. Learning is effective if the student is engaged in the process—and more effective still if the learning takes place collaboratively in a group.

Some people believe that the maker movement began in 1995 at a German organization called C-Base. C-Base was an informal group of people who were interested in hacking—creating—software and hardware. But it really has its origins long before then with various Do It Yourself (DIY) movements, ham radio clubs, quilting clubs, and garage tinkers. Some of these movements were technology oriented, others were workshop oriented. As technology became less expensive and more available, particularly the introduction of 3D printers, colleges and universities began to adopt these resources. It particularly resonated with engineering programs. Only within the past 15 years

---

4   Student-Centered Active Learning Environment for Undergraduate Programs

or so has the maker movement caught on as pedagogy.

At colleges and universities, at its broadest conceptualization, maker space is the merger of seminar space, workshop, computer lab, design studio, and breakout room. The space is sometimes scheduled for credit, more often it is used as an open lab where students make use of the resource on their own time. Although most frequently initiated by engineering programs, these spaces are being developed by the sciences, social science, and humanities programs as well.

In 2014, the White House hosted a Makers Faire where a commitment letter was signed by 150 colleges and universities with existing or planned maker resources. In addition, 130 libraries also signed a commitment letter to advance the Maker Movement. Also participating were a number of corporations and Federal agencies with various announcements of existing or proposed resources to advance and encourage Maker spaces. See the list of institutions at the end of this article.

An intriguing maker space is the Design Lab in the Duderstadt Center at the University of Michigan. It is not a maker space in the traditional sense—although students make things there. The lab itself is designed to change and be rearranged as students and faculty work within the space. The space is informally designed or laid-out into 6 areas with no walls separating the areas: open space, computers, consulting, hangout area, specialized workstations and a messy area. Just about everything is moveable and can be rearranged as needed as student interaction or faculty pedagogy require. It is an open environment and it is just as likely that a course is in process at the same time that other students are in the space working on their own projects.

Another interesting maker space is Georgia Tech's student run Invention Studio which began in 2009 and now consists of 5 rooms of various machines, tools, and technology. The Invention Studio is open to all students. In addition, at least 25 courses had their students use the Studio's resources last year. The rooms vary from a quiet meeting room with computer workstations to a noisy/dusty wood working space, to a welding area, and space for laser cutters, injection molding, and 3D printers and scanners. The Invention Studio has trained technicians/instructors and provides numerous opportunities for hands-on training and educational workshops.

Moving away from engineering for a moment, the University of Mary Washington has a maker space, the ThinkLab, which supports the College of Education and the Division of Teaching and Learning Technologies. The ThinkLab is located within the library, has an array of equipment and high-tech tools for 3D printing, electronics, and robotics. Several courses are taught within the lab, and the space is available for independent student work as well.

Case Western Reserve, with its Think[Box], is creating the largest maker space in the country. It will be a 7 story, 50,000 square foot maker resource that will be available for all departments, students, faculty and staff at the University, as well as a resource for the nearby colleges and universities in Cleveland. The ground floor will be designed for community purposes, workshops, training and meetings for community groups, nearby academic institutions, k-12 students, and corporations. Other floors will be designed for collaboration, prototyping, fabrication, and the staffing and resources to aid in the entrepreneurial process from concept to the market. There will also be space for incubating university and community start-ups. A truly collaborative resource.

Finally, why is DARPA funding maker space at the high school level? DARPA, through its MENTOR program has teamed with Make Magazine and with Otherlab to provide the physical resources to mentor and support the next generation of entrepreneurs and designers. The goal is to establish maker spaces in 1,000 high schools. DARPA's concerns is that the U.S. is losing the ability to invent and to make things. One of the ways to off-set that loss is to reach out to high school students.

This is certainly the time for the maker movement to expand into educational institutions as well as various community centers and forums. These spaces are transforming the way students learn and interact, and hopefully, creating a population unafraid to experiment and create.

List of the 150 institutions that signed a commitment letter at the White House's 2014 Makers Faire

Arizona State University	School of the Art Institute of Chicago
Art Center College of Design	School of the Museum of Fine Arts, School of Visual Arts
Big Bend Community College	Sierra College
Boise State University	South Central College
Boston University	South Mountain Community College
Bucknell University	Spelman College
Bunker Hill Community College	Stanford University
California College of the Arts	State University of New York at New Paltz
California Polytechnic State University	Stevens Institute of Technology
California State University, Northridge	Suffolk County Community College
Cape Cod Community College	Sweet Briar College
Carnegie Mellon University	Tennessee Technological University
Case Western University	Texas A&M University
Catawba Valley Community College	Texas State University
Cerritos College	Tufts University
Charles S. Mott Community College	Tulane University
College for Creative Studies	Tunxis Community College
College of San Mateo	Union College
Columbia University	Union County College
Community College of Allegheny County	The University of Akron
Cornell University	The University of Alabama at Birmingham
Crafton Hills College	The University of Arizona
Cumberland County College	University at Buffalo, The State University of New York
Cuyahoga Community College	University of California, Berkeley
Duke University	University of California, Davis
Eastern Gateway Community College	University of California, Irvine
Eastern West Virginia Community and Technical College	University of California, Los Angeles
Embry-Riddle Aeronautical University	University of California, Merced
Florida International University	University of California, Riverside
Folsom Lake College	University of California, San Diego
Fox Valley Technical College	University of Central Florida
George Mason University	University of Cincinnati, College of Engineering & Applied Science
Georgia Institute of Technology	University of Colorado Boulder
Green River Community College	University of Delaware
Gulf Coast State College	University of the District Columbia
Harvard University	University of Florida
Houston Community College	University of Hawai'i at Mānoa
Howard University	University of Illinois at Chicago
Iowa State University	University of Illinois at Urbana-Champaign
James Madison University	The University of Iowa
Kansas City Art Institute	University of Louisville
Lehigh University	The University of Maryland
LeTourneau University	University of Massachusetts Amherst
Lorain County Community College	University of Massachusetts Lowell
Marshall University	University of Miami
Massachusetts College of Art and Design	University of Michigan
Massachusetts Institute of Technology	University of Michigan-Dearborn
McLennan Community College	University of Minnesota
Michigan State University	University of Missouri System
Mississippi State University	University of New Haven
Monroe Community College	University of North Texas
Morehouse College	University of Notre Dame, College of Engineering
Morgan State University	University of Oregon
New York Institute of Technology	University of Pennsylvania
New York University	University of Pittsburgh
North Carolina Agricultural and Technical State University	University of Pittsburgh at Johnstown
North Carolina State University	University of Portland
Northeast Wisconsin Technical College	University of Southern California, Viterbi Schl of Engineering
Northeastern University	University of St. Thomas
Northern Virginia Community College	The University of Tennessee, Knoxville
Ohio Northern University	The University of Texas at Austin
The Ohio State University	The University of Texas at Dallas
Oregon College of Art and Craft	The University of Texas at El Paso
Oregon Institute of Technology	The University of Toledo
Pacific Northwest College of Art	University of Toronto
Pennsylvania College of Art and Design	The University of Vermont
Pennsylvania State University	University of Washington, College of Engineering
Pennsylvania State University Erie, The Behrend College	Virginia Commonwealth University
Purdue University	Virginia Polytechnic Institute and State University
Rensselaer Polytechnic Institute	Washington University in St. Louis
Rhode Island School of Design	West Virginia University
Robert Morris University	Westmoreland Community College
Rowan University	Wright State University
Rutgers, The State University of New Jersey	Yale University
Saddleback College	Youngstown State University
San Francisco Art Institute	
Santa Clara University	

* * *

"For Want Of A Nail" Campus Planning Without An

Academic Plan is not Planning ~ Arthur J. Lidsky, 2005

Colleges and universities begin a campus planning process for a variety of reasons: a mandate by state agencies, the launch of a capital campaign, a change in management style and culture, the need to select an appropriate site for a new building, a donor or funding organization's requirement, or new administrative leadership. Most often the institution isn't ready to begin a comprehensive campus planning process—but plunges ahead regardless. The most important first step, the academic plan, is typically missing or moribund—and without it, any campus plan is *ad hoc*—and most "campus plans" without the academic plan as the foundation, are simply campus designs.

Comprehensive campus planning integrates three related planning processes: academic, financial, and campus planning. They each inform the other, but the keystone is the academic plan. One reason many institutions do not have an academic plan, or at least not a current plan, is because of the difficulty involved with creating one. It requires serious self-assessment and a vision of the institution's desired future. If done well, the plan will probably require a one- to two- year process that is political, emotional, angst-ridden, and both exciting for some and terrifying for others.

Ideally, the academic plan will have a point of view about enrollment size, faculty distribution, departments to be nurtured, departments to be changed or eliminated, new programs, modified or eliminated programs, current and anticipated research initiatives, and pedagogy. The academic plan should respond to three key questions. Who are our students? What do we want them to know? How do we want them to learn?

One essential element of an academic plan is the definition of strategies for realizing the goals and aspirations articulated in the vision statement. An interesting example that I saw recently had a short mission and vision statement—a paragraph each. The vision statement had seven themes: student retention, for example; and interdisciplinary teaching and research. Each theme had a rationale and a set of goals. For each goal there was a set of strategies for realizing the goal. These strategies had staffing, facilities, operational, and financial implications. This truly helped to guide the financial and campus planning processes that followed.

Another element is the setting of priorities—or not all initiatives of the academic plan can be realized at the same time. Priorities established in the academic plan help structure both the financial and the campus plan.

The academic plan is one of three components of an integrated, comprehensive plan—the other two being financial and campus and facilities.

The financial plan is rooted in the budgetary process and linked to both the academic and campus plans. Operational plans for realizing the strategies articulated in the academic plan need to be created and budgets established. These budgets can be one-year, five-year, and beyond. The financial link to the campus plan is through a capital improvements plan.

Both the operational plans and the budgets should be integrated with the campus plan for capital improvements must be part of the budget and is usually detailed in a capital plan. The capital plan summarizes anticipated costs for new construction, renovation, deferred maintenance, and annual improvements and equipment over a timeline of typically 10 years. The capital plan is a component of the financial plan and it too is dependent on the academic plan for basic assumptions and for future aspirations.

Campus planning is a participatory decision-making process. It must be rooted in an academic plan and fulfill the aspirations expressed in the vision statement. The campus plan is one of the products of campus planning and is the physical form given to the academic and financial plans. The plan melds land, landscape, open space, and buildings; pedestrian and vehicular circulation; topography; codes and standards; utility infrastructure; and history, culture, and politics into two and three-dimensional form designed to reflect and support the vision.

Developing a campus plan without an academic plan will force the institution to make decisions that, while necessary for the plan, will not have been reached through a thoughtful and collegial process. More than likely, the decisions will have been made without the opportunity to build consensus and without the time to analyze the programmatic implications.

Source: Dean & Provost, Volume 6, Issue 7 March 2005
JOSSEY-BASS

PART NINE

STUFF

CHAPTER 9

"Reviewing What We've Learned"

~ Richard P. Dober, 2006

Some recent assignments involving preparing the capital implementation schedule for several campus plans brought to mind once again the necessity of considering the conservation, renovation, and fuller utilization of existing buildings as an alternative to new construction, and the importance of including deferred maintenance in the overall plan.

The mindfulness was prompted by a retrospective review of our work at Oberlin College in 1973. Prodded by a senior administrator who recognized that the seduction of new architecture left the school "space rich but with pockets of poverty all over the campus" and a trustee who argued that the *ad hoc* approach to campus development was not informed stewardship, Oberlin launched a comprehensive review of its physical assets with the objective of having "a cohesive and rational plan."

The proactive approach provided the College with its first comprehensive view of how new and old facilities should be melded into a unified physical development strategy. The planning process also offered those concerned about the decay and neglect of heritage architecture and landscapes an opportunity to advocate for significant investment in the preservation and restoration of landmark facilities. It enabled those responsible for the maintenance and operations of facilities to contribute their experience and knowledge of with local conditions to shape the outcomes.

With the cost of new construction soaring to levels not previously experienced (after discounting inflation), and buildings continuing to age and to become obsolete as they inevitably will, a unified planning outcome is more useful than ever. Accordingly, some version of the Oberlin planning process should be considered, such as the following seven-step study:

1. Organization of the planning effort
2. Description of the existing assets
3. Evaluation of qualitative and quantitative conditions
4. Projection of facility requirements
5. Matching of new and old to meet projected needs
6. Consideration of options
7. Articulation of an implementation plan

Except for situations where life safety or accreditation issues demand immediate remedy, the descriptions of each improvement to be included in the campus plan need not be exact. The objective is to produce an overview that is persuasive as to coverage and inspiring as to the need for implementation.

* * *

"The Financial Crisis" ~ Arthur J. Lidsky, 2009

The economic environment is bleak. Endowments have been reduced, in some instances by one third, and those institutions whose budgets depend on endowment income have been hit hard. Private, tuition driven institutions are seeing students flock to the public sector to find less expensive education. Applications to public colleges and universities are up significantly from the year before as students seek a less expensive education.

Cities and states are seeking financial relief and there will be few educational systems that will be spared from cost reduction.

More than ever before, colleges and universities must act strategically and deliberately. Planning now is essential—not something that is done from time to time—but incorporated into every aspect of campus management.

Any initiative that does not support the mission of the institution should be questioned. "Mission critical" has become a buzz-word— but the concept is important. Those programs and initiatives that are essential to institutional mission should be supported, and those that are not should be questioned, minimized, or eliminated.

Difficult decisions about academic departments and programs must be made. How appropriate is a one or two person department? Can or should any department or program be eliminated?

Can the number of faculty be reduced? As faculty revise retirement plans and opt to continue to work, creating or redefining early retirement incentives will be important. No area should be sacrosanct. The number of administrators and staff should be on the table as well.

Enrollment is another area for assessment. Whereas increasing the enrollment will add income, there are faculty, staff, and facility implications. At what point does increasing enrollment become more costly because of the need to increase the number of faculty or the amount of space? In terms of space, it is not just office and classrooms, it is labs, studios, dining, and residential space that will most likely be affected.

If the number of faculty remain the same and if section size is allowed to grow, are the number and size of existing classrooms, labs, and studios sufficient? It is easier to change utilization than change the number and size of rooms.

Using facilities more effectively is also an effective way to respond to the economic downturn. There are a number of utilization guidelines that can be applied to ensure proper use of classrooms and labs. One common factor addresses the number of hour per week that a classroom is scheduled during the day—30 hours per week. There are several that address how a lab is utilized depending on whether the course is introductory or advanced: 20 hours per week for introductory courses; 12 to 18 hours per week for more advanced courses.

None of this will be easy, but the nation's financial situation gives the institution a chance to realistically think strategically and to realistically assess its mission. Coasting is not an option. Now, more than ever, adjusting programs to mission is a rational approach to survival in the coming years. Setting priorities is a must and creating a plan provides the context for decision makers.

Stetson University
DeLand, FL

* * *

"What's in a Name?" ~ Arthur J. Lidsky, 2009

"What's in a name? That which we call a rose By any other name would smell as sweet." ~ Romeo and Juliet

There are over 3,000 Carnegie halls in the United States—many were designed as libraries or science buildings and many are on college and university campuses. Over time, as institutional needs and programs change, the buildings have changed, but the name remains the same.

At Pomona College, Carnegie Hall is now a humanities and social science building. At Juniata College, Carnegie Library is now a museum and arts building. Allegheny College's Carnegie Hall of Chemistry is now a humanities and social science office and classroom building. And at St. Lawrence University, Carnegie Hall of Science is now home to languages and international programs. What's in a name?

At Carleton College, the Sayles-Hill Gym has been transformed into a student center, and at Wittenberg, Koch Chemistry is now an arts building. What's in a name?

So the name stays the same and functions change. Why would a college or university change its name?

Changing names goes back in time to the original colonial colleges. Of the nine colonial colleges, five have changed their names for a number of reasons—political, donor recognition, and location. The College of New Jersey became Princeton when it relocated the campus from Elizabeth to Princeton, NJ. Kings College became Columbia after an 8 year lacuna of instruction during the Revolutionary War. The College of Philadelphia became the University of Pennsylvania through a more complex series of moves—mostly political. The College was split into two institutions when the State created the University of the State of Pennsylvania. The two were reunited under their present name in 1791. The College of Rhode Island became Brown University when the campus relocated from Warren, RI to Providence and took on the name of a significant donor. Queens College was chartered in 1766 and became Rutgers University in 1825 in honor of the philanthropist Colonel Henry Rutgers.

Usually an institutional name change follows changes in curriculum and program offerings. The typical change is from college to university. Loyola College became Loyola University of Maryland.

Marketing is another reason to change the name. The Boston Architectural Center was an accredited, degree granting institution since the early 1970s—but was largely unknown outside the architectural professional world. The Boston Architectural Club, became the Boston Architectural Center, and just recently became the Boston Architectural College—reflecting what it actually was: an independent, accredited college offering both Bachelor of Architecture (B.Arch), and Master of Architecture (M.Arch) degrees.

Sometimes a change in mission requires a change in name. Florida Junior College at Jacksonville became Florida Community College at Jacksonville in 1986. Recently, it became Florida State University and has expanded their programs and degree offerings and currently serves over 80,000 students on four campuses.

Sometimes, names are changed to avoid confusion. Northface University has changed its name to Neumont University in order to eliminate any confusion with the clothing manufacturer.

Other changes have to do with geography—especially in California where the tradition is to name the campus for the city in which it is located. The California State University, Fullerton El Toro is now CSUF Irvine.

In 1994, Arkansas College became Lyon College to honor a family that was a major supporter of the institution—and to commemorate a significant gift.

The jokes were annoying yet tolerable—although often crude—but their college name became a real problem when internet porn filters stopped campus emails and access to their website. The 150 year old independent women's college in Philadelphia changed their name from Beaver College to Arcadia College.

* * *

"Keeping The Rock Rolling" ~ George G. Mathey, 2009

The past year has been a real wet blanket on the fire that has burned merrily over the past decade driving the engine of campus development. A year in which the key campus development questions have abruptly morphed from "How can we secure that final lead donation for our new facility?" to "How many more people are going to be furloughed or laid off?"

As Arthur wrote in his article " What's in a Name?" down economies can be excellent periods in which to advance transformative strategic planning. In the physical and project planning realm, however, many participants are likely to be asking, "What's the point in planning a new facility or renovation that there's no money to build?" But just as this can be a good time for big picture plans, it's also a good time for pre-architectural project planning. A couple of ideas:

- Convene a group to discuss the next facility called for by your campus plan. Since with tight budgets you are more likely to be doing this in-house, focus the group on the program drivers, rather than the details of facility planning—Why do we need this facility? What strategic goals will it advance? What characteristics can be built into the facility to accomplish those goals? What existing and potential new uses will it accommodate? What principles should guide the reallocation of any space vacated when a new facility comes online? What institution-wide uses or values should it embody? In short, create a vision statement for the building.

- Convene a group to discuss a long-standing, recurring planning concern. Have you been frustrated by the lack of planning guidelines at your institution? Have there been repeated directives to re-imagine the library, or the classroom pool, or departmental office allocation and configuration? Now may be the only time to advance these discussions in a deliberative way.

Take advantage of this time to establish visions and guidelines that can be applied to the next wave of projects you anticipate as the economy improves and feasibility returns.

* * *

"Iconic Qualities" ~ George G. Mathey, 2010

Three of our recent clients have three very different, singular, memorable, iconic main buildings. Each is fulfilling a vital role on its campus and each is at a different stage of its recurring life cycle.

The most typical of the Old Main type, the central portion of St. Charles was the original building for Mount St. Charles College *(see photo 1)*, the precursor to Carroll College. Designed by the Washington D.C.-based A.O. von Herbulis and built in stages from 1909 to 1924, St. Charles is the campus architectural icon, and its palette of red porphyry ashlar blocks with limestone trim and red tile roofs is repeated in several campus buildings. The uses in St. Charles run the gamut from student housing to classrooms, to academic office space to fine arts and music studios to the theatre for the College's thriving performing arts programs (formerly the college gymnasium. The College is working to give St. Charles a first-rate renovation to extend the life of this much-loved symbol of the College.

This neo-classical building *(see photo 2)* designed by Edward Angelo Christy (then architect for the city of New Orleans) and completed in 1921 is both the iconic symbol of the College's City Park campus and its most heavily-used academic and administrative building. Pressed into intensified service in the aftermath of Katrina and the closure of over a third of the campus's facilities, Building 1 houses classrooms, administrative offices, and the departments ranging from Music to Biology to Child Development to ESL to

Theater and the Fitness Center. In order to accommodate accelerating growth (now just shy of pre storm levels) the College is working hard to create new academic space to decompress Building 1 and facilitate renovations that will extend its contributions to the campus and the critical role Delgado is playing in the city's and region's re-building.

Probably the least traditional of the three buildings, this building *(see photo 3)* was designed by Chicago architect George C. Nimmons and began life in 1928 as a Sears Roebuck department store. Acquired by Lesley in 1994, and now re-named University Hall, it currently houses nearly half of the University's classrooms, its science programs, its signature School of Education, as well as a vibrant retail floor at street level to maintain a neighborhood amenity and contribute to the activity in Porter Square.

Although these buildings are very different in history and function each has endured due to some fundamental qualities:

Size—All of these buildings are large, (St. Charles=75,600, Delgado=118,000 NASF, University Hall=166,000 net square feet) making them more accommodating of change, and churn.

Adaptable Structure—Each of these buildings has structural qualities that have ensured longevity and evolutionary capabilities. St. Charles sustained only minor damage to mostly ornamental elements in an earthquake that hit Helena in 1984, and has a robust mixture of large and small spaces to accommodate changing uses. University Hall makes minimal use of bearing walls relying on structural columns that facilitate relatively easy space reconfiguration. Delgado Hall is probably the most structurally constrained, but is at least durable enough to sustain long periods of minimal re-investment. All of the buildings have higher than currently-typical floor-to-floor heights,

Photo 1

St. Charles Hall
Carroll College
Helena, MT

Photo 2

Issac Delgado Hall
(Building 1)
Delgado Community College
New Orleans, LA

Photo 3

University Hall
Lesley University
Cambridge, MA

allowing introduction of systems never contemplated by the original designers and users without compromising the spatial qualities of the rooms.

Campus Heritage—Each of these buildings is the highest profile building on campus and in the case of St. Charles and Delgado Halls, so much of the institution's history is bound to the building that separating the two is nearly impossible. Even University Hall, though a relatively recent acquisition, was instantly the most prominent of Lesley's buildings and connects it most directly to its neighborhood. The very fact of its acquisition sent a signal to the community that Lesley is a dynamic, growing and entrepreneurial institution with a significant public role, symbolizing its transformation into a distinctive University with an enviable national reputation.

Good Esthetics—This is critical. To become an icon, it generally helps to be attractive. None of these buildings are the very best of their types, but all of them evince a refined, handsome presence that speaks to the institution's region, longevity and aspirations.

* * *

"The Library in Transition" ~ Arthur J. Lidsky, 2009

The library—as a symbol, as an academic resource, as a building—is in transition. There may never be a final state for the library as it continues to change in response to many forces. More than any other resource on a campus, the library is changing and must be designed for the incredible change that is occurring as the library evolves from warehousing information to being a river of information and a center for collaboration and interaction.

The quiet, staid building for individual study is morphing into a dynamic, technological collaborative learning and research resource.

LIBRARY USAGE

In general, there is a decline in personal interaction with reference librarians. The first choice for students is to use Google, Yahoo, and other commercial search engines. They are quick, easy, and accessible from anywhere there is a computer.

There is also a general decline in circulation patterns as fewer books are actually checked-out. There is, however, an increase in Inter-Library Loan as libraries broaden their collection by networking with other libraries and share collections.

Nonetheless, the use of libraries on college and university campuses is increasing.

WAREHOUSE TO RIVER

Over time, the rate of library book acquisitions will decline as libraries increase the number of on-line resources, journals, and related databases. There will be books for a long time, but how extensive should the on-site collection be?

Collection management is becoming more important as librarians decide whether a particular book should be maintained on campus or placed in an off-site holding area easily accessible by library staff. A number of libraries are moving books off-site to provide more room for student and faculty study, interaction, and collaboration spaces.

The idea of the library being a warehouse of books is changing as libraries evolve to a more service oriented resource that provides a centralized space for interaction and collaboration.

Is it important for the library to own a book or to provide access to it? As costs go up, more and more libraries are collaborating with other libraries sharing their collections. A specific book can be delivered in hours or a day or two using inter-library loan.

COLLABORATION AND INTERACTION

The advent of the Information Commons is the result of the melding of reference services, information technology, and research on how people learn. The information commons is a computerized space within the library, staffed by both reference librarians and IT professionals skilled in assisting students and faculty in their search for information and knowledge. The information commons is typically a highly active and dynamic space sometimes associated with food services of one type or another—a café, for instance—and usually designed with a number of formal and informal small group meeting spaces, individual study spaces, seminar rooms and places for students to work and study together.

A small group space is typically designed for 4 to 6 students, sitting at a table, with a smart board or white board, computer, projector or wall mounted flat screen, power for laptops, network port, and wireless access. These spaces can be individual rooms with or without doors; they can be alcove spaces, or spaces that use furnishings for visual privacy.

In newly designed buildings, these resources are programmed and designed from the start. In renovated buildings, the need to create these kinds of spaces within the existing building is forcing librarians to look at the size of their collections and to decide the best way to replace book shelves with collaborative spaces for students and library patrons.

College of Saint Benedict
St. Joseph, MN

Spelman College
Atlanta, GA

Corrette Library, Carroll College
Helena, MT

TECHNOLOGY

More than any other factor, the advances, diversity, and rapidity of technological change is changing the library and will continue to change the library. The relation is symbiotic.

The existence of computers in libraries isn't cutting-edge, but an essential resource—whether they are in the information commons, open computer labs, or individual computer workstations distributed throughout the building. Some libraries loan laptops by the hour, day, and week.

Usually the library is both wired and wireless. Some campuses allow guest access to the internet.

Many libraries are creating web access with a consistent interface for the variety of databases that they provide.

Some librarians are advocating for the implementation of Web 2.0 to speed access and ease of use.

An interesting experiment currently in process is the creation of user defined information through blogs, wikis, and instant messaging. Much like Wikipedia, these networks are expanding the scope and extent of information available.

So what should the library of the future look like? No one can predict because it is an ever changing target. It certainly will have books, just fewer. It certainly will have some version of the information commons. It certainly will be a placed for interaction and reflection— for discussion and quiet. It certainly will be a place where technology undergirds student and faculty interaction.

The single most important characteristic of a new library building is the ability to facilitate change: changing technology and infrastructure, changing spaces, and changing human dynamics.

* * *

"The Danger of History Slipping Away"
The Heritage Campus and HBCUs
~ Arthur J. Clement, AIA , Principal, Clement & Wynn, LLC
& Arthur J. Lidsky, 2011

HBCU presidents must learn to use preservation planning as a tool to leverage new resources.

Each year since 1988, the National Trust for Historic Preservation has identified 11 of America's most endangered historic treasures. The list includes individual buildings, landscapes, and whole communities, both urban and rural. The trust explains that "the list spotlights places across America that are threatened by neglect, insufficient funds, inappropriate development, or insensitive public policy" (National Trust for Historic Preservation 2011, ¶ 1). In 1998, 10 years into the program, the National Trust grouped every single Historically Black College and University (HBCU) into one endangered national treasure.

This endangered national treasure is slowly slipping away.

The U.S. General Accounting Office (GAO) (1998) estimated at that time that these HBCUs had 712 buildings in need of restoration and protection at a cost of $755 million. Today, that number would be $1.1 billion, and this assumes low inflation and completed renovation of some buildings during that interval. The GAO also noted that 45.4 percent of the buildings were listed on the National Register of Historic Places and another 28.9 percent were eligible. Thus, nearly 75 percent of the building inventory on HBCU campuses in 1998 was at least 50 years old and historically important. Unfortunately, this endangered national treasure, the cultural resource for many communities across our country, is slowly slipping away.

There are 105 HBCUs in the United States today as defined by the federal Higher Education Act of 1965. There may be additional institutions whose mission and focus is on minority students, but the number of institutions prior to 1964 is set. There will not be any additional HBCUs, but more than likely there will be fewer.

Background

HBCUs are as diverse as higher education. These institutions have different histories, different cultures, and different resources. They are public and private, large and small, two-year and four-year, single sex and coed, religious and non-denominational. The common thread that binds them is their mission to provide access to higher education for African Americans, who were previously enslaved and later segregated in the United States.

The first wave of schools established for freed blacks was started in the North before the Civil War. Due to relocations and other interruptions, many of these schools did not survive, and their successor institutions are no longer connected to their original campuses or historic structures. The next wave of schools was established for recently emancipated slaves and their children in the South following the Civil War. The combined efforts of the Freedmen's Bureau, abolitionist organizations, religious denominations, and local community groups established more than 500 schools across the country (Drewry and Doermann 2001; read chapter 3, "The Beginnings of Black Higher Education" pp. 27–40, for a succinct overview of the early founding of black schools in the United States).

In 1890, Congress passed the second Morrill Act, which stated that blacks were entitled to attend land-grant schools. This ushered in an era of public education for Blacks in segregated schools throughout the southern states. The beginning of the 20th century saw still more schools established for blacks, but by the Great Depression of the 1930s the number of these schools had begun to decline. Many factors contributed to the closings, consolidations, and mergers, including diminished financial support from northern philanthropists and church groups and the rise of accreditation agencies for colleges and universities. During the 1950s and early '60s, some new HBCUs were founded, and there were more mergers and consolidations. Many HBCU campuses were caught up in the civil rights protests of the 1960s, which culminated in the desegregation of public facilities and schools and in the passage of the 1965 Voting Rights Act and the 1965 Higher Education Act.

Current Context

Despite their age, history, and mission—or perhaps because of it—many HBCUs are economically fragile institutions, and the number of failing HBCUs could increase significantly over the next 15 or 20 years. We are in danger of losing an important part of our national history and culture—and more importantly, a valuable educational resource. We are also in danger of losing the buildings and grounds that for decades sustained and nurtured the students, faculty, and staff who made these colleges and universities a vital part of our culture.

In 1966, Congress passed the National Historic Preservation Act (NHPA). This legislation established a framework for preserving the historic fabric of our nation on a local, state, and national level. Since that time, a broader historical perspective has evolved among the agencies that administer the NHPA. The heritage of the United States is now recognized as including a diverse group of ethnic and racial minorities who have left "a rich and varied legacy of accomplishments and historic places that cannot be ignored" (Savage 1994, p. 67). Because of the NHPA, many structures and historic districts on HBCU campuses were recognized as significant and placed on the National Register of Historic Places.

In 1974, a portion of the Tuskegee Institute campus in Alabama was declared a National Historic Site through federal legislation. Subsequently, portions of the Hampton Institute and Fisk University were given status as National Historic Landmarks, followed by the consortium of institutions known as the Atlanta University Center (comprised of Atlanta University, Morehouse College, Spelman College, Clark College, Morris Brown College, and the Interdenominational Theological Center) in 1976. In 1998, the General Accounting Office (GAO) issued a report titled *Historic Preservation: Cost to Restore Historic Properties at Historically Black Colleges and Universities* that listed 54 campuses, slightly more than half of the total count of HBCUs, with historic properties on the National Register (U.S. General Accounting Office 1998). In addition, more than a dozen HBCU buildings were designated as National Historic Landmark sites, including Stone Hall at Atlanta University, Jubilee Hall at Fisk University, Virginia Hall at Hampton University, Hill Hall at Savannah State University, Loockerman Hall at Delaware State University, Swayne Hall at Talladega College, the John Boddie Mansion at Tougaloo College, and Rankin Chapel, Frederick Douglass Memorial Hall, and Founders' Library at Howard University.

In 1988, the National Park Service (NPS) began a program of awarding grants to document, preserve, and stabilize historic structures on HBCU campuses. The first round of grants included funding to rehabilitate 11 historic landmark structures:

- Gaines Hall (North Hall), Morris Brown College, Atlanta, GA
- Leonard Hall, Shaw University, Raleigh, NC
- Hill Hall, Savannah State University, Savannah, GA
- St. Agnes Chapel, St. Augustine's College, Raleigh, NC
- John Boddie Mansion, Tougaloo College, Tougaloo, MS
- White Hall, Bethune-Cookman College, Daytona Beach, FL
- Graves Hall, Morehouse College, Atlanta, GA
- Howard Hall, Howard University, Washington, DC
- Virginia Hall, Hampton University, Hampton, VA
- Packard Hall, Spelman College, Atlanta, GA
- Loockerman Hall, Delaware State University, Dover, DE

According to an October 5, 2010, e-mail message from Linda Hall, NPS grants manager, the NPS HBCU Preservation Program has continued for more than 20 years and has awarded over $40 million in matching grants to more than 60 HBCUs to assist them in repairing historic buildings on their campuses. At first, HBCUs were required to raise 50 percent of the funds locally to match the federal grant. Gradually, the matching requirement was lowered, and in 2009, the American Recovery and Reinvestment Act (ARRA) earmarked $15 million for the NPS budget for the HBCU Preservation Program. The matching fund requirement was lifted to stimulate local economies immediately, and 20 HBCUs received federal grants to stabilize and preserve historic structures on their campuses. The program is expected to be completed in 2012.

The Getty Foundation's Campus Heritage Initiative is part of the Getty Foundation's mission to preserve and conserve the visual arts and architecture. [1] The first grants in this program were awarded in 2002. By 2007, 86 campuses had received grants totaling $13.5 million. The foundation's initiative was "designed to assist colleges and universities in the United States in managing and preserving the integrity of their significant historic buildings, sites, and landscapes. Grants were awarded for projects that focused on the research and survey of historic resources, preparation of preservation master plans, and development of detailed conservation assessments" (J. Paul Getty Trust n.d., ¶ 6).

In 2002, Spelman College was the first HBCU to receive a Campus Heritage Initiative grant. Others soon followed, and by 2007, eight more HBCUs were awarded grants:

- Bennett College, Greensboro, NC
- Clark Atlanta University, Atlanta, GA
- Dillard University, New Orleans, LA
- Morehouse College, Atlanta, GA
- Talladega College, Talladega, AL
- Tougaloo University, Jackson, MS
- Tuskegee University, Tuskegee, AL
- Virginia Union University, Richmond, VA

The grant enabled an institution to document its historic resources, assess conditions, and develop guidelines for treatment that would serve as a basis for future conservation and rehabilitation projects. The grant required a final report, and most of these documents are now posted online at the Campus Heritage Network website (www.campusheritage.org) sponsored by the Society for College and

University Planning. The Campus Heritage Network serves as an online exchange for preservation planning.

The campus heritage plan for Spelman College analyzed and recommended preservation strategies for 14 historic buildings that form the campus core, from Rockefeller Hall (constructed in 1886) to Abbey Rockefeller Hall (constructed in 1952). The landscape treatment for the historic Campus Oval was also described in the report. In addition, the planning team worked with the college's archivist to catalogue numerous historic photographs and original blueprints, which are now stored in the archives. Spelman is fortunate to have maintained its original campus grounds since 1884, and it has continuously occupied and preserved the original cluster of buildings that encircles the Campus Oval (figure 1). Since the completion of the plan, Spelman has rehabilitated three of its core structures: Sisters Chapel, Packard Hall, and Rockefeller Hall, and has received historic preservation awards for each project.

Clark Atlanta University (CAU) is the merger of two institutions: Atlanta University (established in 1865 and later chartered in 1867) and Clark College (established in 1869). The CAU campus heritage plan analyzed 14 buildings and included a pictorial report on the original campuses of both schools prior to their 1988 merger. The report included North Hall (constructed in 1869), Stone Hall (1883), Knowles Industrial Building (1884), Oglethorpe School (1905), and Kresge Hall (1954, built on the historic Clark College residential quadrangle). Treatment recommendations were developed for the academic quadrangle of Atlanta University and the residential quadrangle of Clark College (figure 2). Given the institution's varied history and multiple campus locations, the plan has become an

Figure 1: Spelman College Campus Oval

Plan of Campus Oval

HISTORIC BUILDINGS

Rockefeller Hall, 1886 (1)
Packard Hall, 1888 (2)
Giles Hall, 1893 (3)
Reynolds Cottage, 1901 (4)
Morehouse James Hall, 1901 (5)
MacVicar Hall, 1901 (6)

Physical Plant, 1901 (7)
Upton Hall, 1907, demolished (8)
Bessie Strong Hall, 1917 (9)
Laura Spelman Hall, 1918 (10)
Tapley Hall, 1925 (11)
Sisters Chapel, 1927 (12)

Aerial of Campus Oval – circa 1930s

Aerial of Campus Oval – January 2007

Images courtesy of Spelman College Archives

Figure 2: Clark Atlanta University Historic Quadrangles

Residential Quadrangle

Image courtesy of the Robert W. Woodruff Library Special Collections, Atlanta University Center

Academic Quadrangle

important reference guide. Since the plan was finished, five building renovations have been completed, including one project that received an award for historic preservation and one that received LEED Silver certification. CAU was also a recipient of a 2009 ARRA NPS HBCU grant for Trevor Arnett, the first library building constructed on the consolidated Atlanta University Center campus in 1932.

At Bennett College for Women, the campus heritage plan analyzed and assessed 12 buildings constructed between 1915 and 1941. The plan described the historic campus landscape and the boundaries within the 25-acre core and developed recommendations that guided five subsequent building renovations, including the adaptation of the original 1927 heating plant into an academic facility for the English and Journalism Department. In addition, the grant funded the creation of an educational brochure on DVD illustrating the pictorial history of the college and the evolution of its historic campus. The recording included a description of many of the campus's heritage components: the Bennett Bell, the Bearden Gates, and the original trees planted on the main quadrangle, which were severely damaged during a major storm. In 2009, Bennett College for Women received an ARRA NPS HBCU Preservation Grant to stabilize Black Hall, constructed in 1936 as its first science building, and to make the building handicapped accessible.

Dillard University's campus heritage plan developed building assessments and preservation recommendations for 13 historic buildings from Rosenwald Hall (1934) to the Alexander Library (1960). Also included was an off-campus hospital, Flint-Goodrich, designed and constructed in an Art Deco style in 1932 that served the African American community in New Orleans for decades. Unfortunately, the hospital is now closed and the facility has been converted into housing for seniors. Dillard is blessed with stunning campus grounds, including the beautiful Rosa Keller Avenue of the Oaks (figure 3). Landscape treatments for the broad lawns, the oaks, and other historic open spaces were defined and described in the plan. In late August of 2005, Hurricane Katrina caused widespread flooding throughout the city of New Orleans, and Dillard's campus was inundated with water. The Dillard campus heritage plan was an invaluable record of existing building conditions that was used to assist in the reconstruction of the historic structures that suffered extensive wind and water damage. Dillard was a recipient of a 2009 ARRA NPS HBCU Preservation Grant for Camphor and Hartzell Halls, two dormitories within the historic core campus.

The Morehouse College campus heritage plan studied six historic buildings that form the main core of the campus, ranging from Samuel Graves Hall (1890) to Danforth Chapel (1955). The plan recommendations defined the landscape treatment and surface water drainage system for the main campus quadrangle. Since the plan was finished, Morehouse has concentrated on constructing new facilities in its outlying campus precincts and has not conducted a major renovation project within its historic core.

Founded in 1867, Talladega College is Alabama's oldest historically Black liberal arts college. Its campus heritage plan focused on a select group of buildings that had been placed on the National Register in 1990 as part of the Talladega College Historic District. The beauty of the college's landscape, with its towering, mature oak trees scattered throughout the campus, creates a pastoral setting that impresses students and visitors from the moment they arrive. A central portion of the plan surveyed the historic landscapes by campus area, assessed their

Figure 3: Dillard University Avenue of the Oaks

Rosa Freeman Keller
Avenue of the Oaks
(1936 & 2006)

Images courtesy of Dillard University Archives

Figure 4: Fort Valley State University Aerial Campus Views

North and Middle Campus – 1972

North Campus – 2007   **South Campus – 2009**

Images courtesy of Fort Valley State University Archives

character-defining features, and made treatment recommendations for preserving the natural settings. Talladega's campus contains a wide variety of architectural building styles, ranging from the majestic Greek Revival Swayne Hall (a National Landmark structure), to the Romanesque Revival Deforest Chapel, to modest 20th-century frame-constructed faculty houses, to the Collegiate Gothic Savery Library built during the late 1930s, to a modern international-style administration building of the late 1950s. Talladega's environs tell the story of how small HBCUs have struggled valiantly for more than 140 years in the Deep South against overwhelming odds. In 2009, Talladega received an ARRA HBCU Preservation Grant for Foster Hall, constructed in 1870 as the first women's dormitory and later expanded in 1903. The building was vacant and boarded up prior to the grant. The college is now energized to seek additional funding to complete the restoration of this historic structure and re-open the building as a residence hall.

In 2003, the Getty Foundation awarded a grant for $180,000 to the University System of Georgia (USG) to develop a template and set of guidelines for creating a campus historic preservation plan that could be integrated into the campus master planning process on its 35 campuses. One campus was used initially to shape the template and to codify a set of guidelines for the process. By 2007, USG was ready to develop a campus historic preservation plan for two of its HBCUs, Fort Valley State University and Savannah State University. The two colleges presented two different challenges in terms of preserving their campus settings and histories.

Savannah State was the first public HBCU in the state of Georgia, founded in 1890. Set near the coast just outside of Savannah, the campus was developed on two former antebellum plantations. Over time, many of the original wood-frame plantation buildings were demolished and replaced during the 1930s with brick structures in a Georgian Revival style. Although the campus had expanded greatly, a significant portion of the historic core remained intact, including the imposing Hill Hall, a masonry building built with student labor around the turn of the 20th century. Savannah State wanted its campus historic preservation plan to assess and preserve the early campus heritage resources and to recommend a historic district for nomination to the National Register.

Fort Valley State University was founded in 1895 and existed until 1939 as a private, segregated high school with a focus on industrial education for blacks living in the middle counties of the state of Georgia. While a private high school, Fort Valley State constructed a cluster of buildings grouped around a central quadrangle on the north end of its campus. This historic core was placed on the National Register in 2000. Following its conversion to a state-supported public land-grant institution for blacks in 1939, the university's middle campus developed over the late 1940s, '50s, and '60s. Over the ensuing decades, Fort Valley State grew to become the second largest campus in terms of land area in the USG. The expansive growth pulled Fort Valley State further away from its historic core and middle campus, articularly following the development of a new student housing complex and academic buildings at the south end of the campus (figure 4). The campus historic preservation team was charged with making recommendations for how best to connect the three campus sectors while preserving the heritage elements of an agricultural land-grant institution.

Michael Miller, a preservation architect who worked in the USG Real Estate and Facilities Office, supervised the campus historic preservation plan process for both Fort Valley State and Savannah State. Miller reported that a direct outcome of the Fort Valley State campus historic preservation plan was board approval of an updated campus master plan that recommended preserving and repurposing the buildings in the middle campus (pers. comm.). (The previous master plan called for demolishing many of these buildings.) Two of the oldest campus buildings that were vacant received funding for rehabilitation. The first structure, Huntington Hall (built in 1908), received an NPS HBCU Preservation Grant in 2007 and a matching grant from the state legislature to rehabilitate the building as offices for the president and his senior staff. The second structure, Ohio Hall, was assessed and treatment strategies were devised during the campus historic preservation plan study. The Georgia state legislature and USG Board of Regents appropriated funding for the rehabilitation of Ohio Hall as a student residence hall two years later. At Savannah State, the state legislature and Board of Regents approved funding for renovating several of the historic buildings on the core campus in conjunction with a new student housing development proposed next to Hill Hall, a National Historic Landmark structure. According to Miller, the campus historic preservation plan reports have given the college presidents a new tool to use in the capital planning process by finding new purposes for old buildings that embody the cultural heritage of their respective campus (pers. comm.).

The Closing of Doors

Over the years, a number of HBCUs have closed their doors and no longer exist. Reasons cited for the closings range from loss of accreditation to inadequate financial resources, low student enrollment, and weak leadership. These institutions have gone out of business, merged with other HBCUs, or partnered with a majority institution. Unfortunately, their campuses and buildings were then left in limbo along with the overhanging debt and hurt feelings of alumni and friends. In a few cases, new owners have stepped forward to repurpose the campuses and buildings. A short list of institutions that have closed their doors includes:

- Bishop College, 1881–1988 (Dallas, TX)
- Knoxville College, 1875–2007 (Knoxville, TN)
- Daniel Payne College, 1889–1979 (Birmingham, AL)
- Mary Holmes College, 1892–2005 (West Point, MS)
- Morris Brown College, 1881– (Atlanta, GA)
- Mount Hermon Female Seminary, 1875–1924 (Clinton, MS)
- Storer College, 1865–1955 (Harpers Ferry, WV; campus is now maintained as a part of the Harpers Ferry National Historic Park)
- Bricks College, 1906–1931 (Whitakers, NC; now the Franklinton Center operated by the United Church of Christ)
- Palmer Memorial Institute, 1901–1971 (Sedalia, NC; now a State Historic Park called the Charlotte Hawkins Brown Historical Site)

Four examples are discussed in more detail to highlight the challenges of repurposing campuses that have closed or are marginally operational. Mary Holmes College, Bishop College, and Storer College are examples of campuses successfully readapted to new uses. The Morris Brown College campus, near the edge of downtown Atlanta, has yet to find a new use for its vacant and deteriorating historic buildings. When HBCUs close their doors, what happens to the cultural resources of these institutions? How are the stories and traditions preserved along with the remaining buildings?

For Mary Holmes College, a two-year college in Mississippi, the immediate cause for closing was financial. At the April 2004 trustees meeting, the board voted to seek bankruptcy. The college was on probation with the Southern Association of Colleges and Schools (SACS) and had failed to meet its enrollment goals. The Presbyterian Church USA (PCUSA), which owned the land, supported the college as it struggled for survival and through the bankruptcy process. In the end, the church decided to sell the 184-acre campus along with its 23 college buildings.

PCUSA's goal was to sell the property to an educational buyer or to one associated with social justice or women's issues. It took six years and six offers before the campus was finally sold to the Regional Foundation for Mental Health and Mental Retardation, Inc. Initial plans are to renovate and reuse many of the buildings for administration, patient care, and a museum that focuses on the history of Mary Holmes College.

Bishop College in Dallas, Texas, is an example of an HBCU that closed its doors after 107 years of operation. Its buildings and campus were acquired by another HBCU, Paul Quinn College.

Bishop was founded in 1881 by the Baptist Home Mission Society in Marshall, Texas, and moved to its new campus in Dallas in 1961. Although the college was historic, its campus and buildings were only 50 years old. Bishop struggled financially for years. A charge of embezzlement, the loss of SACS accreditation, and declining enrollments brought the college to an end. Since acquiring the campus, Paul Quinn College has demolished several buildings and is restoring several others.

Yet, the spirit of Bishop endures through the Bishop College Heritage Preservation Foundation, Inc. Established in March 2010 as a 501(c)(3) charitable organization, the foundation's mission is to "protect the heritage of Bishop College and preserve its reputation of academic rigor through the Bishop College Alive! Scholarship program in partnership with Georgetown (KY) College" (Bishop College Heritage Preservation Foundation, Inc. 2010, ¶ 2).

Storer College was founded in 1865 at the end of the Civil War and closed in 1955. No longer an educational institution, it is still educating as part of the Harpers Ferry National Historical Park, which has preserved and repurposed the college's buildings and campus for the National Park Service.

Storer has been inextricably involved in the history of this country: Harpers Ferry, Fredrick Douglass, John Brown, and the powerful forces that emerged after the failure of reconstruction. Begun as a primary school by the Freewill Baptist Home Mission Society, Storer then became a normal school to provide teachers for the large number of freed slaves who hungered for an education. In 1938, the school became a college, fulfilling the goal of the institution's major donor, John Storer, who gave the first large gift in 1868.

Morris Brown College was once a proud member of the Atlanta University Center. Today, the fate of this historic church-related school hangs by a slender thread. Enrollment has declined from 3,000 students to approximately 70, and the number of faculty has decreased from more than 100 to fewer than 10. The college is deep in debt. One of its former presidents pleaded guilty to embezzlement of federal loan funds and served a year of home confinement (Haines 2011). SACS withdrew its accreditation from Morris Brown College in 2003, and with it went federal funding for Title III dollars and Pell grants for student aid. The college also lost the support of the United Negro College Fund and was ejected from the Atlanta University Center corporation. Without this crucial network of support, Morris Brown College is virtually closed.

What will happen to this historic campus and the landmark buildings that comprise the original site for Atlanta University? Perhaps the National Park Service will acquire them, much as it did with Storer College at Harpers Ferry, and repurpose them into a park to interpret and celebrate the story of African American higher education and the civil rights movement that arose on many of the HBCU campuses. Someone has suggested that the college be reborn as a residential college, much like Oxford University. Others have suggested that the remaining five institutions of the Atlanta University Center absorb and re-use the remaining academic, residential, and athletic facilities.

Today, the former Atlanta University campus and its historic buildings lay idle, and the proud vision expressed by W. E. B. Du Bois (1903) of an emerging university on one of the thousand hills of Atlanta producing a talented generation of new leaders to lift the black race up from bondage lies in ruins.

A Message to HBCU Presidents

On many campuses in the United States, the buildings and land are worth more than the institution's financial endowment. Yet the physical environment is often placed low on the priority list of needs. Meanwhile, the financial assets that comprise the endowment are fretted over and measured annually by consultants—every effort is made to increase their value.

An educational institution has many conflicting needs and

priorities, and by postponing improvements to the physical plant, emphasis can be shifted to the academic program or to student life. It is a matter of survival.

Unfortunately, buildings deteriorate over time through constant use. The cost of deferring maintenance increase over the years. Many HBCUs, with only modest financial resources, have found themselves in this situation.

Campuses with historic buildings are in a double bind. First, they have been entrusted with the stewardship of these culturally and architecturally significant buildings without the resources to care for them. Second, these buildings, many ranging from 70 to 100 years old, are often no longer suitable for current use and are in some cases vacant. They have become eyesores on the campus. Additionally, many buildings constructed during the 1960s and '70s with low-cost government loans are now aging and in desperate need of updating and repair. These buildings are actively used, but are woefully lacking in new instructional technology and do not comply with current building codes.

What should a president do?

One of the chief roles of a college president is to plan for the future of the institution and to articulate a vision that is large enough to embrace both the academic challenges of the 21st century and the urgent need to protect, enhance, and celebrate the campus resources of the previous century. For HBCU presidents, the tension is more acute as they struggle to balance a strategic plan for the future with the burden of maintaining a unique campus heritage, all within an annual operations and capital budget of insufficient revenues and resources.

A college president must adopt a mindset that incorporates a strategic planning and leadership style that becomes an integral part of how the college operates on a day-to-day basis. Planning must be continuous and ongoing, not sporadic or only done on a schedule—or not done at all.

Comprehensive campus planning integrates enrollment planning, financial planning, facility and campus planning, residential life planning, and the most important planning of all—academic planning. Based on these planning initiatives, a series of needs can be identified and prioritized. The highest priority are those needs that support the institution's mission and vision and that are urgent. The lowest priority are those needs that are benign to the mission and vision and that can be accomplished at any time.

Alternatives can then be developed that address the college or university's needs, and then the costs and benefits of each alternative can be weighed. If done properly, the alternatives will have programmatic, financial, staffing, and facility implications. Campus heritage issues and opportunities can be identified and specific requirements and treatment strategies attached to certain buildings or sectors of the campus (Dober 2005). From this process, a comprehensive campus plan will emerge.

Also, a separate campus heritage plan should be developed that focuses solely on the cultural resources of the institution, including those historic properties that are representative of the institution's DNA—its unique legacy and mission. Once this plan is finished, its recommendations must be integrated into the overall institutional campus plan and strategic vision so they become a part of all future capital planning decisions.

Why do more than half of all HBCUs not take advantage of the federal and foundation grants available for historic preservation? One answer is probably the lack of financial resources and technical assistance needed to do the preliminary planning and assessment required to document the significance of a historic property, to get it nominated to the National Register, and to propose treatment recommendations that comply with Department of the Interior standards.

Another answer may be that the president has acknowledged that the task of restoring a historic building is too daunting and prefers to focus his or her energies on developing a new facility that will become a legacy for the current administration.

As the examples described in this article show, HBCUs cannot afford to ignore two important sources of funding. One is the National Park Service HBCU Preservation Program, and the other is the Getty Foundation. But to qualify for either program, the HBCU must have an eligible property or historic district listed on the National Register. Once this prerequisite is met, the key is to seek out grants to cover the upfront planning and assessment work and then leverage these initial grants into larger capital dollars from other funding sources. Several HBCUs highlighted in this article have followed this approach.

There are a number of national foundations that might provide funding, including the Kresge Foundation, the National Science Foundation, the Pew Charitable Trusts, and the Bush Foundation. Both the Kresge and Bush foundations have a history of working with HBCUs. In addition to the national foundations, there are hundreds of local foundations in cities and states throughout the country that might be interested in assisting with historic preservation once grants have been received from the larger foundations.

Conclusion

HBCU presidents must learn to use preservation planning as a tool to leverage new resources, new partnerships, and new grant funding. They should encourage their senior staff to look for creative ways to attract foundation grants for preservation and sustainability as well as federal grants for maintaining and readapting older properties for new uses. Integrating a historic core campus closely interwoven with the legacy of the institution is a successful way to build broad support among incoming students, alumni, and local community leaders.

The early buildings, open spaces, and campuses that date back to the period of segregation when the majority of HBCUs were founded are deserving of historic preservation and ongoing public support. HBCUs tell the broader history of the United States and reflect the growing cultural pluralism of the country and its rich tapestry of ethnic and geographic diversity. HBCUs are part and parcel of the ongoing struggle for African Americans to gain access to education, to receive training for professional jobs, to achieve a middle-class existence, and to carry the banner for social justice, civil rights, and human rights for all Americans.

References:

Bishop College Heritage Preservation Foundation, Inc. 2010. Bishop Foundation Flyer. Retrieved January 19, 2011, from the World Wide Web: www.bishopcollegefoundation.org /Bishop_Foundation_Flyer.pdf.

Dober, R. P. 2005. Campus Heritage. Ann Arbor, MI: Society for College and University Planning.

Drewry, H. N., and H. Doermann. 2001. Stand and Prosper: Private Black Colleges and Their Students. Princeton, NJ: Princeton University Press.

Du Bois, W. E. B. 1903. The Souls of Black Folk. Chicago: A. C. McClurg & Co.

Haines, E. 2011. Ex-Morris Brown College Leader Recounts Her Ruin. Atlanta Journal Constitution, Jan. 11.

J. Paul Getty Trust. n.d. Previous Initiatives. Retrieved January 19, 2011, from the World Wide Web: www.getty.edu/foundation /funding/conservation/previous/index.html.

National Trust for Historic Preservation. 2011. America's 11 Most Endangered Historic Places. Retrieved January 19, 2011, from the World Wide Web: www.preservationnation.org/issues /11-most-endangered.

Savage, B. L., ed. 1994. African American Historic Places. New York: John Wiley & Sons.

U.S. General Accounting Office. 1998. Historic Preservation: Cost to Restore Historic Properties at Historically Black Colleges and Universities. GAO/RCED-98-51, Report to Congressional Requesters. Washington, DC: U.S. General Accounting Office.

Note

[1] The individual college and university grant reports referenced in this article completed as part of the Getty Foundation's Campus Heritage Initiative can be found at www.campusheritage.org.

Source:

Society for College and University Planning (SCUP), Planning for Higher Education, April-June 2011

THE END

ABOUT THE AUTHORS

Arthur J. Lidsky, AICP, FAAAS
President, DOBER LIDSKY MATHEY

Arthur became president of DOBER LIDSKY MATHEY in 1988, and has served as a planning consultant for colleges and universities since 1971. In this time he has participated in several hundred assignments. For the three years prior to his consulting work, he was Assistant Director of Long-range Planning for the Massachusetts Institute of Technology.

Arthur has served on facility review panels for the National Science Foundation (NSF). He has given lectures, presentations, and invited papers on campus planning at such organizations as SCUP, the Council for Undergraduate Research (CUR), the International Association for College Unions, No Name Facility Conference, Quality Education for Minorities Network (QEM), and the Municipal

Art Society of New York. He had been a faculty member of Project Kaleidoscope for more than a decade, and has been the only non-institutional member on the PKAL National Steering Committee.

Through his writing and lectures, Arthur teaches other professionals, college and university administrators, and faculty about planning and the campus planning process. He has taught campus planning as a faculty member of SCUP's Integrated Planning Institute and was a leader in creating the Institute and its curriculum. Arthur has contributed articles to numerous professional publications, including his most recent seven; The Journal of the New England Board of Higher Education, New Directions for Higher Education, Facilities Manager, Dean & Provost, The Chronicle of Higher Education, College Planning and Management, Planning Higher Education. He was awarded SCUP's Founder's Award and is a Fellow in the American Association for the Advancement of Science.

George G. Mathey, AICP

Principal, DOBER LIDSKY MATHEY

George, a key member of the firm since 1986, became a principal at DOBER LIDSKY MATHEY in 2002. Over these years, he has participated in more than 121 planning assignments for DLM's college and university clients. Through his work on 49 campus planning studies, and 72 facility planning studies, he has developed a particular strength in space utilization; space needs projection (the translation of strategic goals to space requirements), and facility programming. While much of his work is with small liberal arts institutions, George has also been involved in all of DLM's international projects over the past decade as well as in work with the largest research university clients, gaining a broad perspective of a wide range of campus planning and space needs issues.

George shares his experience with others through seminars and presentations to students and practitioners. The most recent of these was a seminar to a class at MIT on facility programming, a presentation at the 2013 annual meeting of the Society for College and University Planning on Implementing Strategic Planning through Space Planning", one in 2007 on "Facility Programming for Sustainability" and another at the 2002 meeting on the topic, "The US News & World Report's Rankings and Institutional Space Resources".

A selection of recent projects George has contributed to include: campus planning for Belmont Hill School, Carroll College, Cyprus

International University, Delgado Community College, Harvard Graduate School of Education, Harvard Department of Athletics, Harvard School of Public Health, Lesley University, Morehouse School of Medicine, and The College of Wooster; space utilization studies for Cornell University; existing space analysis and space needs projection for the Connecticut State University system, Massachusetts College of Art and Design, the Ohio State University, the University of Hong Kong, University of Massachusetts-Lowell, Westfield State University; and facility programming for the sciences at Holyoke Community College, Marist College, Tri-County Technical College, and for the new campus of the American University in Cairo, Egypt.

www.dlmplanners.com